Lecture Notes in Computer Science   10953

Commenced Publication in 1973
Founding and Former Series Editors:
Gerhard Goos, Juris Hartmanis, and Jan van Leeuwen

More information about this series at http://www.springer.com/series/7407

Mathias Payer · Awais Rashid
Jose M. Such (Eds.)

Engineering Secure Software and Systems

10th International Symposium, ESSoS 2018
Paris, France, June 26–27, 2018
Proceedings

 Springer

Editors
Mathias Payer
Purdue University
West Lafayette
USA

Jose M. Such
King's College London
London
UK

Awais Rashid
University of Bristol
Clifton
UK

ISSN 0302-9743 ISSN 1611-3349 (electronic)
Lecture Notes in Computer Science
ISBN 978-3-319-94495-1 ISBN 978-3-319-94496-8 (eBook)
https://doi.org/10.1007/978-3-319-94496-8

Library of Congress Control Number: 2018947337

LNCS Sublibrary: SL1 – Theoretical Computer Science and General Issues

This Springer imprint is published by the registered company Springer International Publishing AG part of Springer Nature
The registered company address is: Gewerbestrasse 11, 6330 Cham, Switzerland

Preface

It is our pleasure to welcome you to the proceedings of the 10th International Symposium on Engineering Secure Software and Systems (ESSoS 2018), co-located with the conference on Detection of Intrusions and Malware & Vulnerability Assessment (DIMVA 2018). ESSoS is part of a maturing series of symposia that attempts to bridge the gap between the software engineering and security scientific communities with the goal of supporting secure software development. The parallel technical sponsorship from ACM SIGSAC (the ACM interest group in security) and ACM SIGSOFT (the ACM interest group in software engineering) demonstrates the support from both communities and the need for providing such a bridge.

Security mechanisms and the act of software development usually go hand in hand. It is generally not enough to ensure correct functioning of the security mechanisms used. They cannot be blindly inserted into a security-critical system, but the overall system development must take security aspects into account in a coherent way. Building trustworthy components does not suffice, since the interconnections and interactions of components play a significant role in trustworthiness. Lastly, while functional requirements are generally analyzed carefully in systems development, security considerations often arise after the fact. Adding security as an afterthought, however, often leads to problems. Ad Hoc development can lead to the deployment of systems that do not satisfy important security requirements. Thus, a sound methodology supporting secure systems development is needed. The presentations and associated publications at ESSoS 2018 contribute to this goal in several directions: first, by improving methodologies for secure software engineering (such as flow analysis and policy compliance). Second, with results for the detection and analysis of software vulnerabilities and the attacks they enable. Finally, for securing software for specific application domains (such as mobile devices and access control).

The conference program featured two keynotes, as well as research and idea papers. In response to the call for papers, 26 papers were submitted. The Program Committee selected seven full-paper contributions, presenting new research results on engineering secure software and systems. In addition, three idea papers were selected, giving a concise account of new ideas in the early stages of research. ESSoS received four requests for artifact evaluation, out of which three were evaluated correctly and received the artifact evaluation badge. Many individuals and organizations contributed to the success of this event. First of all, we would like to express our appreciation to the authors of the submitted papers and to the Program Committee members and external reviewers, who provided timely and relevant reviews. Many thanks go to the Artifact Evaluation Committee for assessing the quality of the submitted artifacts to the Steering Committee for supporting this series of symposia, and to all the members of the Organizing Committee for their tremendous work. We are thankful to ACM SIGSAC/SIGSOFT and LNCS for continuing to support us in this series of symposia.

The engineering of secure software and systems in an increasingly hyperconnected world is both a major challenge and a fundamental need to ensure that the digital fabric underpinning our society remains resilient in the face of a variety of threats. Bringing researchers from software and systems engineering and computer security to discuss challenges and solutions is an important important step in this regard. It has been our pleasure to chair the program for ESSoS 2018.

May 2018   Mathias Payer
                                                                        Awais Rashid

Organization

Steering Committee

Jorge Cuellar	Siemens AG, Germany
Wouter Joosen (Chair)	KU Leuven University, Belgium
Fabio Massacci	University of Trento, Italy
Bashar Nuseibeh	The Open University and LERO, UK
Juan Caballero	IMDEA Software Institute, Spain
Eric Bodden	University of Paderborn, Germany
Lorenzo Cavallaro	Royal Holloway University of London, UK

Organizing Committee

Program Co-chairs

Mathias Payer	Purdue University, USA
Awais Rashid	University of Bristol, UK

Publication Chair

Jose M. Such	King's College London, UK

Publicity Chair

Raoul Strackx	KU Leuven University, Belgium

Local Organizers

Sebastien Bardin	CEA, France
Gregory Blanc	Telecom SudParis, France

Web Chair

Annick Vandijck	KU Leuven University, Belgium

Program Committee

Yasmin Acar	Leibniz University Hannover, Germany
Luca Allodi	Technical University of Eindhoven, The Netherlands
Pauline Anthonysamy	Google Inc., Switzerland
Rakesh Bobba	Oregon State University, USA
Alvaro Cardenas	The University of Texas at Dallas, USA
Lorenzo Cavallaro	Royal Holloway University of London, UK

Tom Chothia   University of Birmingham, UK
Sven Dietrich   The City University of New York, USA
Mattia Fazzini   Georgia Institute of Technology, Atlanta, USA
Yanick Fratantonio   EURECOM, France
Seda Gurses   Princeton University, USA
Marina Krotofil   FireEye, Inc., USA
Per Larsen   University of California, Irvine, USA
Martina Lindorfer   University of California, Santa Barbara, USA
Mira Mezini   Technical University of Darmstadt, Germany
Nick Nikiforakis   Stony Brook University, New York, USA
Michael Pradel   Technical University of Darmstadt, Germany
Kaveh Razavi   ETH Zurich, Switzerland and Vrije Universiteit Amsterdam,
                             The Netherlands
Abhik   National University of Singapore, Singapore
  Roychoudhury
Riccardo Scandariato   University of Gothenburg, Sweden
Laurie Williams   North Carolina State University, USA

Artifact Evaluation Committee

Lieven Desmet   KU Leuven, Belgium
Sylvain Frey   Google DeepMind
Joseph Hallett   University of Bristol, UK
Jan Tobias   KU Leuven, Belgium
  Muehlberg

Additional Reviewers

Sarah Elder
Sylvain Frey
Andrei Homescu
Trishank Karthik
Raul Quinonez
Akond Rahman
Chris Theisen

Contents

A Vision for Enhancing Security of Cryptography in Executables

Otto Brechelmacher, Willibald Krenn, and Thorsten Tarrach(✉)

AIT Austrian Institute of Technology, Giefinggasse 4, 1210 Vienna, Austria
thorsten.tarrach@ait.ac.at

Abstract. This paper proposes an idea on how to use existing techniques from late stage software customization to improve the security of software employing cryptographic functions. In our vision, we can verify an implemented algorithm and replace it with a faster or more trusted implementation if necessary. We also want to be able to add encryption to binaries that currently do not employ any, or gain access to unencrypted data if an application depends on encryption.

To corroborate the feasibility of our vision, we developed a prototype that is able to identify cryptographic functions in highly optimized binary code and tests the identified functions for functional correctness, potentially also revealing backdoors.

1 Introduction

In recent years cryptography became almost universal in applications, both commercial and open-source. Every application securely communicating with its cloud server relies on a full suite of symmetric and asymmetric encryption algorithms. Hence, running a closed-source application employing cryptography requires one to trust the software developer to (a) consistently use cryptography, (b) have chosen a good crypto-library and use it correctly, and (c) not to have built-in a backdoor that leaks sensitive information.

Especially when dealing with software running in a sensitive environment it is necessary to thoroughly inspect the software for potential vulnerabilities and threats. We focus on the correctness analysis of the software using the binary code as unwanted functionality can be introduced during the compilation process [1], the original source code or libraries are not available, or one cannot re-produce bit-matching binary images from the supplied sources. For similar reasons, i.e. no source available or highest level of trust, any late stage customization has to be performed on the machine-code level. In the following, we focus on cryptography routines because they are often exposed to the network and present a major part of the attack surface of an application. Also, this specific domain allows us to use a lot of domain-specific knowledge in the attempted automated analysis.

The research leading to this paper has received funding from the AMASS project (H2020-ECSEL no. 692474).

M. Payer et al. (Eds.): ESSoS 2018, LNCS 10953, pp. 1–8, 2018.
https://doi.org/10.1007/978-3-319-94496-8_1

Once some piece of software fails the verification, information about vulnerabilities becomes public, or encryption needs to be added due to changing security requirements, the software needs to be patched or replaced. In order to save on the re-certification/verification effort, we propose to automatically address the shortcomings in the binary file. Put differently, we do not only want to analyze binaries, but also fix certain problems automatically or even add encryption to binaries that do not currently employ encryption, e.g. adding HTTPS to a legacy application.

While one source of vulnerabilities are sophisticated, deliberate backdoors, we believe a significant portion of flaws are accidental. Developers typically are not very knowledgeable in cryptography. A common pattern these days is that developers use the first seemingly working code-snipped from some blog or stack-exchange answer for their code. There are numerous problems when using cryptography in this naïve way.

The first problem is that developers may use a home-grown implementation of their desired cipher or some not very well maintained library. Such home-grown implementations will not contain hardening against side-channel attacks and will likely contain unknown bugs or weaknesses [2]. The second problem is connected to the use of statically linked libraries. Here, one issue is that the user of the software cannot easily update the version of the library used, once a vulnerability has been found. Further, the user has no guarantees (and is generally unable to check) whether the software supplier has used the latest version of the library when building the release. As security issues are regularly found and fixed in libraries, this is a major problem. Lastly, even the best crypto library may be used incorrectly. There are numerous topics around encryption, such as key management or safe storage and erasure of the key in memory that a developer can get wrong.

In the past numerous flaws concerning cryptography have been found in software. Here are some of the more interesting cases. Our first example has been revealed by the Chaos Computer Club of Germany (CCC) in software used by the German government to spy on suspected criminals. On close analysis of the software, which is also known as the federal trojan horse, the CCC discovered that the trojan used the same hard-coded AES-key to secure the data transfer to the control server for years. The key can now be found on the internet [3]. Hence, unauthorized parties would have been able read the data transferred. The second example is the well-known Heartbleed bug [4]. This bug may still be present in applications that were statically linked with any of the vulnerable OpenSSL versions. Here, we would want an automated upgrade of the library linked into the affected applications to fix the issue. A third example shows another source for weaknesses when using cryptographic functions: the random number generator. The best crypto implementation does not help if the key is predictable. This was the case in Debian's OpenSSL package, that was able to generate only 32 768 different keys [5]. As before, we would like to be able to address this bug by replacing the random generator used in the application by a trusted one. These are just a few examples, but they illustrate a need to focus on cryptography as part of a software security analysis and life cycle. They also show that binary analysis is needed because merely analyzing the input and output of the application may not reveal a faulty crypto implementation.

We are now ready to present our vision in Sect. 2, before arguing for its feasibility in Sect. 3 by presenting already existing work we can build on. Finally, we conclude this idea paper in Sect. 4.

2 The Vision

As we have shown in Sect. 1, the current treatment of cryptography in the life-cycle of executable programs is far from optimal. Put shortly, the user has no efficient way of checking whether the employed algorithms or library versions are up-to-date, whether the cryptographic primitives are used correctly, or whether the advertised algorithms are used at all. Even worse, once vulnerabilities are discovered there is no easy way to fix the affected executables. Finally, there is no way to add additional functionality to the application.

Our vision is to address these shortcomings with a platform for analyzing, rewriting, and embedding cryptographic functions in binaries. By 'binary' we mean a compiled program, where we don't have access to the source code or any debug information. We understand the term cryptography here in its wider sense to also include random number generators needed to generate keys, cipher modes (counter mode, cipher feedback mode, etc.), and cryptographic protocols like TLS. We envision our platform to have the following features:

- **Analyze** cryptographic functions in the binary for correctness and potential backdoors. The analysis should reveal if the algorithm computes the correct result, has potential information leaks, and if it is vulnerable to known attacks.
- **Replace** cryptographic functions in the binary with alternate implementations.
- **Insert** cryptographic functionality, which is most useful for legacy binaries.

While these features seem trivial, achieving them is far from it. We will use a few scenarios to illustrate common problems and how our platform would help.

Unknown Binary Using Crypto. Assuming we bought an application that employs the Advanced Encryption Standard (AES) according to the data sheet. In this situation we need to check whether AES really is being used and whether there are (known) vulnerabilities, weaknesses, or leaks with this version. Hence in this scenario we could use the analysis capabilities of our platform. In case we are not satisfied with the quality of the implementation, we can then replace the existing AES implementation with calls to our own trusted library.

Legacy Application Without Patches. Another important situation is the maintenance of legacy applications without vendor support. Be it a statically linked application or an application dynamically linked to some outdated version of some cryptographic library that contains known vulnerabilities. In order to develop our own patch for the application, our platform can be used. In the case of an statically linked application, the platform will supply the means to replace the original library version with an updated one. If the application has a dynamic dependency one might be able to find a drop-in replacement if the interface did not change. If, however, there was some interface change, our platform will help with its insert and replacement functionality to add adapter code so the application can use the interface incompatible new version of the library.

Adding Encryption. A further use case we envision for our platform is to add encryption to executables. This could be done by adding transient encryption/decryption when saving/loading files but could also mean securing network connections in non-standard ways. For example we may want to enable a legacy application to encrypt its network traffic. The encryption could be added to the data passed to the send function of libc and the decryption to the data returned by the receive function. We could provide standard packages that also take care of key derivation between peer, for example as part of the connect call. Similarly employing steganography or adding direct support for onion routing techniques would benefit from our platform.

Weakening Encryption. While not in our primary focus, our platform could even be used to weaken a cryptographic implementation. This could be useful in case of reverse engineering, i.e. malware analysis. An important part of reverse engineering is the network traffic, which may be difficult to analyze if it is TLS encrypted with certificate pinning. Our framework would save the analyst a lot of time by simply leaking the encryption key to a file.

All of the discussed scenarios can be realized manually with dedicated personnel. Our platform, however, should automate the work involved as much as possible. While this is no easy feat, we think it is viable and give an overview of already available building blocks in the following section.

3   Available Already

Quite a number of building blocks for our vision are already in place. On the one hand there is a large body of research and tools that deal with binary analysis and manipulation, on the other hand we started working towards our platform for Linux/x86-64 and gained first, encouraging results.

In the following sub-sections, we give a brief overview of available tools and techniques that help realizing our vision. Starting from tools helping with binary rewriting and analysis, we refer to techniques used for specifying machine code that needs replacement before describing our own contributions.

3.1 Supporting Tools

Binary Rewriting. We benefit from a large body of work in runtime manipulation of machine code and binary rewriting. We use DynamoRIO [6] to inject code and modify the control flow of binaries during runtime. While this is ideal for prototyping we would eventually want to rewrite the binaries to persist changes in it. Rewriting binaries is challenging because the control flow can be unpredictable due to exceptions and signals and because some parts of the code may be only revealed at runtime due to Just-In-Time compilation or encryption. Thankfully many of these problem are already addressed, e.g. in Zipr++ [7] and RL-Bin [8].

Binary Analysis. There are two approaches to analyzing a binary. One is to observe the binary during its normal operation at runtime. That is suitable to understand the normal operation of the binary, but not to find a backdoor. The latter can be found for example by symbolic analysis, a technique to reach all program locations. The downside is that such analysis is inherently slow. Since we expect the crypto routines to be part of the normal operation of the binary our prototype uses runtime analysis. We use DynamoRIO to record a trace that we later analyze. A trace means the sequence of all machine code instructions that were executed during a single run of the binary under observation.

There are a few symbolic analysis frameworks for machine code, including S2E [9], angr [10], and libtriton [11]. We also showed that it is feasible to use KLEE [12] for symbolic analysis if the machine code is first lifted to LLVM intermediate language. A task that is non-trivial in itself and we completed only for simple binaries.

Specification. We specify functions and their input/output behavior with the help of model programs. That means we have a model of the intended functionality as a specification and are searching for functions that, when given the same input, will return the same value. Hence our specification does not use pairs of inputs and outputs, but a reference implementation of the function we are looking for. To our knowledge this specification approach is novel in the field.

Another specification method is to use seed functions [13]. Seed functions are functions in the binary one wants to remove by removing the function and all functions that depend on it. These functions can specify a function in a specific binary, but cannot describe the same functionality over all binaries. An alternative is dual slicing [14] where a feature is defined by the difference in two program executions. So the program is started with two different parameters and the function calls that are present in only one trace are the functions of interest.

3.2 First Results

Using these building blocks we built a prototype demonstrating parts of our vision.

Identification. Our specification is given in the form of an implementation of the crypto functions we are looking for. We use these to find the functions of interest in the trace we recorded. The naïve approach of testing all functions called in the trace brute-force does not scale. We therefore employ domain-knowledge to narrow the search: A candidate function can often be identified by its use of certain constants (SBox in AES), specific CPU instructions (AES-NI), or heuristically by a density of bit-level operations in the code. To test the latter we use a machine-learning approach that is able to identify functions containing cryptographic operations with high confidence. A different approach is implemented in CryptoHunt [15] and the Software Analysis Workbench [16], where the authors translate the binary program into logical formulas that can be compared to a given reference implementation with an SMT solver.

Function identification is further complicated because we also need the order of parameters of the function in order to replace or invoke it. Again a brute-force attempt would be very slow, so we again use domain knowledge: The parameters we are interested in (plaintext, key, ciphertext) are pointers to memory buffers of at least 16 byte length. That significantly reduces the number of parameters we need to test.

Testing Cryptographic Implementations. Knowing the exact interface we can test the cryptographic implementation in the binary. We support two test modes:

Firstly, we support supervised encryption, which means that we check after every invocation of the encryption routine if the returned result is correct. This is done by running in parallel a trusted implementation. At this point we could also replace the entire crypto routine with the trusted implementation. Currently this check is done at runtime using DynamoRIO.

The second test mode is to run the encryption function against a list of well-known input-output pairs. In case of AES such pairs are provided by the NIST [17]. This works during runtime by waiting until the encryption function is first invoked and then repeatedly invoking just the encryption function with the chosen inputs and comparing the outputs to the specified ones. Any deviation is an indication that the encryption is not implemented correctly. This is essentially a from of differential testing [18].

Symbolic Analysis. We already use symbolic analysis to find so-called logic bombs in binaries. A logic bomb is a malicious action hidden in the binary and triggered on certain conditions. In terms of crypto this could for example be a backdoor leaking the key. A first attempt working on source code was already published [19] and we are currently busy porting this to the machine code level.

Replacing the Encryption Algorithm. The identification of the encryption algorithm and its parameters is the first important step to allow replacing the encryption algorithm. Our framework could be trivially extended to make the replacement at runtime with DynamoRIO. This is because we already intercept the call to crypto functions for testing. Instead of running both functions and comparing the result, one could simply return the result of the reference implementation and never invoke the original function. While the runtime manipulation of the binary is perfect for testing, it is not desirable as a permanent solution due to the overhead. Therefore we need the binary rewriting tools outlined in Sect. 3.1 to persist changes in the binary itself.

Inserting Encryption. To insert encryption we need to specify insertion points, e.g. function calls to libc. libc is a standard C library used by virtually every Linux application. We can replace these calls with a transparent wrapper to encrypt data before it is passed to libc and decrypting data returned by libc. This could be done when writing data to a file or to a network socket. Of course this would be further complicated by adding key management and exchange. To protect the keys in memory from the original application we can use novel CPU-backed technologies that isolate certain parts of memory, such as Intel SGX.

3.3   Evaluation

Our current prototype implements the complete testing toolchain for AES: It has the ability to record traces, find the addresses and parameters of the crypto functions, and test the crypto function using NIST vectors. We implemented several models for AES using two modes (ECB and CTR) and various keylengths.

We can not only process the small toy examples we created for numerous ways to implement AES, but also the aescrypt2 sample program from the mbedTLS library [20]. All these example were compiled with GCC optimization level 3 and without symbols. The aescrypt2 example is 180 kb in size and contains more than 7000 assembler instructions.

4   Conclusion

We have presented our vision on how to address the challenges posed by cryptography in the life-cycle of executable programs. In order to automate the process of testing and adapting executables as much as possible, we propose to build a platform capable of analyzing, replacing, and inserting cryptographic functions with the goal of achieving a high level of automation. For this, we rely on a mix of techniques known from binary analysis and rewriting, program verification, model-based testing, and compiler construction.

Our envisioned platform will help analysts find flawed cryptographic implementations and replace them by trusted ones or even insert encryption functionality into executable programs. We have made promising first steps towards our vision by implementing parts of the platform on the Linux-x86-64 platform and applying it to different applications relying on AES. Our lessons learnt led us to new approaches for speeding up solving the identification problem of functions and parameters, which we are implementing right now. We are also working on improving the symbolic analysis to make it more scalable and applicable to larger executables. Finally, we want to use rewriting techniques to make permanent changes to binaries as the next step in going after our vision.

References

1. Thompson, K.: Reflections on trusting trust. Commun. ACM **27**(8), 761–763 (1984)
2. Egele, M., Brumley, D., Fratantonio, Y., Kruegel, C.: An empirical study of cryptographic misuse in Android applications. In: CCS 2013, pp. 73–84 (2013)
3. CCC: Analyse einer Regierungs-Malware. Technical report, Chaos Computer Club (2011)
4. Codenomicon, Google-Security: CVE-2014-0160. Available from MITRE, CVE-ID CVE-2014-0160, 3 Dec 2013
5. Bello, L.: CVE-2008-0166. Available from MITRE, CVE-ID CVE-2008-0166, 9 Jan 2008
6. Bruening, D., Zhao, Q., Amarasinghe, S.: Transparent dynamic instrumentation. ACM SIGPLAN Not. **47**(7), 133–144 (2012)
7. Hiser, J., Nguyen-Tuong, A., Hawkins, W., McGill, M., Co, M., Davidson, J.: Zipr++: exceptional binary rewriting. In: FEAST 2017, pp. 9–15 (2017)
8. Majlesi-Kupaei, A., Kim, D., Anand, K., ElWazeer, K., Barua, R.: RL-Bin, robust low-overhead binary rewriter. In: FEAST 2017, pp. 17–22 (2017)
9. Chipounov, V., Kuznetsov, V., Candea, G.: The S2E platform: design, implementation, and applications. TOCS **30**(1), 2 (2012)
10. Shoshitaishvili, Y., Wang, R., Salls, C., Stephens, N., Polino, M., Dutcher, A., Grosen, J., Feng, S., Hauser, C., Kruegel, C., Vigna, G.: SoK: (state of) the art of war: offensive techniques in binary analysis. In: S&P 2016 (2016)
11. Saudel, F., Salwan, J.: Triton: a dynamic symbolic execution framework. In: Symposium sur la sécurité des Technologies de l'information et des Communications, SSTIC, France, Rennes, June 3–5 2015, SSTIC, pp. 31–54 (2015)
12. Cadar, C., Dunbar, D., Engler, D.R., et al.: KLEE: unassisted and automatic generation of high-coverage tests for complex systems programs. In: OSDI. vol. 8, pp. 209–224 (2008)
13. Jiang, Y., Zhang, C., Wu, D., Liu, P.: Feature-based software customization: preliminary analysis, formalization, and methods. In: HASE 2016, pp. 122–131 (2016)
14. Kim, D., Sumner, W.N., Zhang, X., Xu, D., Agrawal, H.: Reuse-oriented reverse engineering of functional components from x86 binaries. In: ICSE 2014, pp. 1128–1139 (2014)
15. Xu, D., Ming, J., Wu, D.: Cryptographic function detection in obfuscated binaries via bit-precise symbolic loop mapping. In: S&P 2017, pp. 921–937 (2017)
16. Dockins, R., Foltzer, A., Hendrix, J., Huffman, B., McNamee, D., Tomb, A.: Constructing semantic models of programs with the software analysis workbench. In: VSTTE 2016, pp. 56–72 (2016)
17. Bassham III, L.E.: The advanced encryption standard algorithm validation suite (AESAVS). NIST Information Technology Laboratory (2002)
18. McKeeman, W.M.: Differential testing for software. Digit. Techn. J. **10**(1), 100–107 (1998)
19. Papp, D., Buttyán, L., Ma, Z.: Towards semi-automated detection of trigger-based behavior for software security assurance. In: SAW 2018 (2018)
20. ARM: mbedTLS. https://tls.mbed.org/

Enforcing Full-Stack Memory-Safety in Cyber-Physical Systems

Eyasu Getahun Chekole[1,2]($\boxtimes$), Sudipta Chattopadhyay[1], Martín Ochoa[1,3], and Guo Huaqun[2]

[1] Singapore University of Technology and Design, Singapore, Singapore
eyasu_chekole@mymail.sutd.edu.sg
[2] Institute for Infocomm Research (I2R), Singapore, Singapore
[3] Department of Applied Mathematics and Computer Science,
Universidad del Rosario, Bogotá, Colombia

Abstract. Memory-safety attacks are one of the most critical threats against Cyber-Physical Systems (CPS). As opposed to mainstream systems, CPS often impose stringent timing constraints. Given such timing constraints, how can we protect CPS from memory-safety attacks? In this paper, we propose a full-stack memory-safety attack detection method to address this challenge. We also quantify the notion of tolerability of memory-safety overheads (MSO) in terms of the expected real-time constraints of a typical CPS. We implemented and evaluated our proposed solution on a real-world Secure Water Treatment (SWaT) testbed. Concretely, we show that our proposed solution incurs a memory-safety overhead of 419.91 μs, which is tolerable for the real-time constraints imposed by the SWaT system. Additionally, We also discuss how different parameters of a typical CPS will impact the execution time of the CPS computational logic and memory safety overhead.

1 Introduction

Cyber-physical systems [1–3], which integrate computations and communications with physical processes, are gaining attention and being widely adopted in various application areas including power grid, water systems, transportation, manufacturing, healthcare services and robotics, among others. Despite their importance, two major issues have raised concerns about the safety of CPS in general. On the one hand, the increasing prevalence of cyber attacks poses a serious security risk; on the other hand, real-time requirements and legacy hardware/software limit the practicality of certain security solutions available. Thus, the trade-off between security, performance and cost remains one of the main design challenges for CPS.

In this paper, we focus on memory-safety attacks against computing nodes of a CPS. These attacks typically are launched on programmable logic controllers (PLCs) and exploit memory-safety vulnerabilities. Most PLCs nowadays are user-mode applications running on top of a POSIX-like OS, often Linux

© Springer International Publishing AG, part of Springer Nature 2018
M. Payer et al. (Eds.): ESSoS 2018, LNCS 10953, pp. 9–26, 2018.
https://doi.org/10.1007/978-3-319-94496-8_2

OS. Therefore, memory-safety vulnerabilities may be discovered on the PLC firmware and control software (*user-space*) or the Linux kernel (*kernel-space*). For example, a malware can corrupt the memory of the PLC or the kernel to hijack or otherwise subvert its operations.

Memory-safety vulnerabilities arise due to the use of programming languages where memory management is handled manually, such as C/C++. Those languages are particularly relevant in systems with stringent real-time constraints since they allow skilled programmers to produce efficient compiled code. However, since firmwares of PLCs and operating systems are commonly implemented in memory-unsafe languages (for the sake of efficiency), the memory unsafety remains a significant security concern. For instance, buffer overflows and dangling pointers, are regularly discovered and reported in modern PLCs.

Common Vulnerabilities and Exposures (CVE) [4] have been reported for a wide-range of memory-safety vulnerabilities only on PLCs for the last couple of decades. For example, a buffer overflow vulnerability concerns Allen-Bradley's RSLogix Micro Starter Lite (CVE-2016-5814) [5]. This allows remote attackers to execute arbitrary code via a crafted rich site on summary (RSS) project file. Yet other buffer overflow vulnerabilities are reported on this PLC [6,7]. Similarly, CVEs are also recently reported for memory-safety vulnerabilities discovered on Siemens PLC [8,9], Schneider Electric Modicon PLC [10,11], ABB PLC automation [12], and so on. Recent CVE reports also show a high volume of interest in exploiting the Linux kernel [13].

Existing countermeasures against memory-safety attacks [14–26] face several challenges to be employed in the context of CPS. First, almost all of them have architectural compatibility problems in working with PLCs, because the PLCs are often based on RISC-based ARM or AVR CPU architectures. More fundamentally, the countermeasures have non-negligible runtime overheads, which may unacceptably compromise the performance of a CPS. Violation of timing constraints in a CPS may lead to serious consequences, including complete system damage or disruption and incorrect control by the use of stale information. Hence, vis-a-vis the exploitation concerns, performance and availability are equally critical in a CPS environment.

To cover a wide range of memory-safety errors, the code-instrumentation based countermeasures, which we refer to as memory-safety tools, offer stronger guarantees. These tools detect memory-safety violations before the attackers get a chance to exploit them. Although there are published benchmarks for the overheads caused by such tools, which give an intuition of average penalties to be paid when using them, it is still unclear how they perform in a CPS context.

In this paper, we leverage memory-safety compilation tools ASan [20] (for the user-space) and KASan [27] (for the kernel-space) to enforce full-stack memory safety in CPS. We quantify the performance impact of our solution via an empirical approach that measures the memory-safety overhead. We evaluated our approach on SWaT [28], a realistic CPS water treatment testbed that contains a set of real-world vendor-supplied PLCs. However, the PLC firmware for the SWaT is closed-source and hence, it does not allow us to incorporate additional memory-safety solutions. To circumvent this challenge, we prototyped an experimental setup, which we call open-SWaT, based on open-source PLCs and mimic the behavior of the SWaT according to its detailed operational profile. Our experiments on open-SWaT reveal that the introduced memory-safety overhead would not impact the normal operation of SWaT.

In summary, this work tackles the problem of *quantifying the practical tolerability of a strong full-stack memory-safety enforcement on realistic Cyber-Physical Systems with hard real-time constraints and limited computational power.*

We make the following contributions: **(a)** We enforce a full-stack memory-safety countermeasure based on memory-safe compilation for a realistic CPS environment. **(b)** We empirically measure and quantify the tolerability of the induced overhead of the countermeasure based on the real-time constraints of a real industrial control system. **(c)** We discuss parameters that affect the absolute overhead to generalize our observations on tolerability beyond our case study.

2 Background

In this section, we provide background information on cyber-physical systems, the CPS testbed we use for experimentation (SWaT) and the memory-safety tools we enforced to our CPS design (ASan and KASan).

2.1 Overview of CPS

CPS constitute complex interactions between entities in physical space and cyber space. Unlike traditional IT systems, these complex interactions are achieved through communication between physical world via sensors and digital world via controllers (PLCs) and other embedded devices. A general architecture of CPS and the interactions among its entities is shown on Fig. 2 (in Appendix). Since these systems are real-time, there are latency and reliability constraints. If these real-time constraints are not met, system could run in to an unstable and unsafe state. The devices in a typical CPS are resource constrained too. For example, PLCs and I/O devices have limited memory and computational power. In general, a typical CPS consists of the following entities:

- *Plants:* Entities where physical processes take place.
- *Sensors:* Devices that observe or measure state information of plants and physical processes which will be used as inputs for controllers (PLCs).
- *PLCs:* Entities that make decisions and issue control commands (based on inputs obtained from sensors) to control plants.
- *Actuators:* Entities that implement control commands issued by PLCs.
- *Communication networks:* Communication medias where packets (containing sensor measurements, control commands, alarms, diagnostic information, etc.) transmit over from one entity to another.
- *SCADA:* A software entity designed for process controlling and monitoring. It consists of human-machine interface (HMI) – for displaying state information of plants – and historian server (for storing all operating data and alarm history).

2.2   Overview of SWaT

SWaT [28] is a fully operational water purification plant designed for research in the design of secure cyber physical systems. It produces 5 gal/min of doubly filtered water.

Purification Process. The whole water purification process is carried out by six distinct, but cooperative, sub-processes. Each process is controlled by an independent PLC (details can be found on [29]).

Components and Specifications. The design of SWaT consists of various components such as real-world PLCs to control the water purification process; a remote input/output (RIO) terminal consisting of digital inputs (DI), digital outputs (DO) and analog inputs (AI); a SCADA system to provide users a local system supervisory and controls; a complex control program written in ladder logic; and so on. It also consists of various system specifications such as a real-time constraints and communication frequencies with other PLCs and the SCADA system. A detailed account of the components and specifications is provided in our previous work [30].

2.3   ASan

As discussed on the introduction, despite several memory-safety tools being available, there applicability in the CPS environment is limited due to compatibility and performance reasons. After researching and experimenting on various memory-safety tools, we chose ASan [20] (for the user-space enforcement) as a basis for our empirical study because of its error coverage, high detection accuracy and relatively low runtime overhead when compared to other code-instrumentation based tools. A detailed account on error coverage and runtime overhead of ASan (in comparison with other tools) is provided on [20,31].

ASan is a compile-time code instrumentation memory-safety tool. It inserts memory-safety checks into the program code at compile-time, and it detects and mitigates memory-safety violations at runtime. ASan covers several memory-safety vulnerabilities such as buffer overflows, dangling pointers (use-after-free), use-after-return, memory leaks and initialization order bugs. Although there are also some memory errors, e.g., uninitialized memory reads, that are not covered by ASan, such errors are less critical and rarely exploited in practice.

Similar to other memory-safety tools, the off-the-shelf ASan has compatibility issues with RISC-based ARM or AVR based architectures. ASan has also a problem of dynamically linking shared libraries, e.g., *glibc*, for our experimental setup. Therefore, as explained on Sect. 4.1, our initial task was fixing those problems to fit our experimental design. For this task it was crucial that ASan is an open-source project, which allowed for several customizations.

2.4 KASan

KASan [27,32] is a fast and dynamic memory error detector tool mainly designed for the Linux kernel. It is also a compile-time code instrumentation memory-safety tool. However, KASan is designed to cover only buffer overflows and dangling pointers not to significantly affect the performance of Linux kernel. Consequently, its runtime overhead is considerably low when compared to ASan. Several kernel memory bugs have been already detected using KASan [33]. Therefore, we chose KASan for the kernel-space enforcement. The current version of KASan is supported only for the x86_64 and ARM64 architectures. Hence, it has compatibility issue with ARM32 architecture, which we have fixed it. As discussed on Sect. 6.2, the practical tolerability of its overhead (together with ASan) is also evaluated against the real-time constraints of SWaT.

3 Attacker Model and Memory Safety Overhead

In this section, we will introduce our attacker model and formulate its implication in computing memory-safety overheads and its tolerability.

3.1 Attacker Model

Memory-safety attacks, such as code injection and code reuse, mainly exploit memory-safety vulnerabilities in the firmware, control software or OS kernel of PLCs. Figure 2 (in Appendix) shows an architectural point of view of memory-safety attacks in CPS. In general, we consider the following five steps involved in a memory-safety attack scenario:

1. Interacting with the victim PLC, e.g., via network connection.
2. Finding a memory-safety vulnerability (e.g. buffer overflow) in the firmware, control software or the OS kernel with the objective of exploiting it.
3. Triggering a memory-safety violation on the PLC, e.g., overflowing a buffer.
4. Overwriting critical addresses of the vulnerable program, e.g., overwriting return address of the PLC program.
5. Using the new return address, diverting control flow of the program to an injected (malicious) code (code injection attacks) or to existing modules of the vulnerable program (code reuse attacks). In the former case, the attacker can get control of the PLC with its injected code. In the latter case, the attacker needs to collect appropriate gadgets from the program, then she will synthesize a shellcode that will allow her to get control of the PLC.

3.2 Modeling Memory Safety Overhead

To ensure memory-safety, firmware and control software of a PLC and kernel of the hosting OS should be compiled with a memory-safety tool. Hence the memory-safety overhead (MSO) will be added to the execution time of the PLC. PLCs handle two main processes – a communication process and a scan cycle process. The communication process handles any network communication related tasks, e.g., creating connections with communicating entities and receiving and sending network requests. The scan cycle thread handles the main PLC process that involves three operations: scanning inputs, executing the underlying control program and updating outputs. The PLC scan cycle starts by reading the state of all inputs from sensors and storing them to the PLC input buffer. Then, it will execute the control program of the PLC and issue control commands according to the state of sensor inputs. The scan cycle will be concluded by updating output values to the output buffer and sending control commands to the actuators.

The measurement of the actual time elapsed by the PLC scan process, i.e., the time elapsed to scan inputs, execute the PLC program and update outputs is reflected via scan time (T_s). By hardening the PLC with memory-safety protection, we also increase the scan time, which is attributed to the memory safety overhead. Concretely, the memory safety overhead is computed as follows:

$$MSO = \hat{T}_s - T_s, \tag{1}$$

where $\hat{T}_s$ and T_s are scan time with and without memory-safe compilation, respectively. A detailed account of modeling T_s is provided in our earlier work [30].

3.3   Quantifying Tolerability

A typical CPS involves hard real-time constraints. With memory-safe compilation, we introduce additional overhead, specifically increasing the scan time of a PLC (cf. Eq. (1)). We define the notion of tolerability to check whether the induced overhead by the memory-safe compilation still satisfies the real-time constraints imposed by the CPS.

Concretely, a typical scan cycle of the PLC must be completed within the duration of the specified cycle time (T_c). We define two notions of tolerability – (1) for average-case and (2) for the worst-case. In particular, after enabling memory-safe compilation, we compute the scan time (i.e., $\hat{T}_s$) for n different measurements and compute the respective average and worst-case scan time. Formally, we say that the MSO is tolerable in average-case if the following condition is satisfied:

$$\frac{\sum_{i=1}^{n} \hat{T}_s(i)}{n} \leq T_c \tag{2}$$

In a similar fashion, MSO is tolerable in the worst-case with the following condition:

$$\max_{i=1}^{n} \hat{T}_s(i) \leq T_c \tag{3}$$

where $\hat{T}_s(i)$ captures the scan time for the i-th measurement after the memory-safe compilation.

4   Enforcing Full-Stack Memory-Safety

It is often mistakenly believed that there is no operating system in PLCs. Most PLCs today are just user-mode applications running on top of POSIX-like operating systems such as Linux OS. For example, Allen-Bradley PLC5 has *Microware OS-9* [34]; Allen-Bradley Controllogix has *VxWorks* [34]; Schneider Quantum has *VxWorks* [34]; Emerson DeltaV has *VxWorks* [34]; LinPAC has *Linux OS* [35]; OpenPLC has *Linux OS* [36]; User-programmable Linux® controllers has *Linux OS* [37]; and so on. Thus, the PLCs work as a software stack running on top of the underlying OS. Therefore, the overall architecture of the control system consists of two main parts: the application stack (that includes the PLC firmware and control software) and the underlying OS.

As discussed in the introduction, the PLC firmware and the control software might have memory-safety vulnerabilities as they are often written in C/C++ due to performance reasons. As such, memory-safety attacks could exploit such vulnerabilities to attack PLCs. Similarly, operating systems are also often implemented in C/C++, hence they might also have memory-safety vulnerabilities. For example, a VxWorks vulnerability (reported on US-CERT [38]) affected Rockwell and Siemens products. Therefore, memory-safety attacks could also exploit vulnerabilities on the operating systems. In particular, attacks could exceptionally target vulnerabilities in the kernel (as also recent trends show in CVE [13]); because the kernel is the core of the machine's OS that is responsible for several critical tasks, e.g. memory management, CPU allocation, system calls, input/output handling, and so on.

To address these security concerns, we proposed a full-stack memory-safety solution that comprises a *user-space* and *kernel-space* memory-safety enforcements. The former refers a memory-safety enforcement to the PLC firmware and control software whereas the later refers a memory-safety enforcement to the OS kernel where the PLC is running on. In this research work, we use Open-PLC controller [36] – a software stack running on top of Linux OS – and the following sections discuss how we enforced the two memory-safety solutions.

4.1   Enforcing User-Space Memory-Safety

As stated on the introduction, our approach to counter memory-safety attacks at user-space level is by secure compiling of the PLCs' firmware and control software. We ported ASan for that, but porting ASan to our CPS design was not a straightforward task because of its compatibility and dynamic library linking problems. Thus, we fixed those problems by modifying and rebuilding its source code and by enabling dynamic library linking runtime options.

To do the secure compilation, we also need to integrate ASan with a native C/C++ compiler. Fortunately, ASan can work with GCC or CLANG with a `-fsanitize=address` switch – a compiler flag that enables ASan at compile time. Therefore, we compiled our OpenPLC firmware ad control software using GCC with ASan enabled.

4.2 Enforcing Kernel-Space Memory-Safety

As discussed on Sect. 2.4, KASan [27] is a memory-safety tool designed for the Linux kernel. Therefore, we compiled the Raspberry PI Linux kernel (where our controller is running on) with KASan to detect kernel-level memory-safety violations, such as buffer overflows and dangling pointers. To do so, we configure the kernel with a `KASAN=y` configuration option. But, doing so was not also a straightforward task because of an architectural comparability problem to work on a 32-bit Raspbian kernel. Because KASan is designed only for the x86-64 and ARM64 architectures. To solve the problem, we did a custom kernel build by cross-compiling with a 64-bit Linux OS.

4.3 Detection and Mitigation

As discussed on Sects. 2.3 and 2.4, ASan and KASan instrument the protected program to ensure that memory access instructions never read or write the so called "poisoned" redzones [20]. Redzones are small regions of memory inserted in between any two stack, heap or global objects. Since the program should never address them, access to them indicates an illegal behavior and it will be considered as a memory-safety violation. This policy detects sequential buffer over/underflows, and some of the more sophisticated pointer corruption bugs such as dangling pointers (use-after-free) and use-after-return bugs (see the full list on Table 3). With the ASan enforcement, we detected two global buffer overflow vulnerabilities on the OpenPLC Modbus implementation.

The mitigation approach of ASan and KASan is based on the principle of "automatically aborting" the vulnerable program whenever a memory-safety violation is detected. It is effective in restricting memory-safety attacks not to exploit the vulnerabilities. However, this approach might not be acceptable in a CPS environment since it highly affects availability of the system and leaves the control system in an unsafe state. Thus, we are currently working on a different mitigation approach to address these limitations.

5 Experimental Design

Unfortunately, SWaT is based on closed-source proprietary Allen Bradely PLCs, hence we cannot modify their firmware to enforce memory-safety solutions. Thus, we designed open-SWaT – a mini CPS based on open source PLCs that mimics features and behaviors of SWaT. By doing so, we managed to conduct our experiment on realistic and closed-source proprietary PLCs, indirectly. We discussed design details of open-SWaT in the following sections.

5.1 open-SWaT

open-SWaT is designed using OpenPLC [36] – an open source PLC for industrial control systems. With open-SWaT, we reproduce operational details of SWaT;

in particular we reproduce the main factors (mentioned on Sect. 6.4) that have significant impact on the scan time and MSO. In general, the design of open-SWaT consists of the following details.

PLCs: we designed the PLCs using OpenPLC controller that runs on top of Linux on Raspberry PI. To reproduce hardware specifications of SWaT PLCs, we specified 200 MHz fixed CPU speed and 2Mb user memory for our PLCs.

RIO: we use Arduino Mega as RIO terminal. It has AVR based processor with 16 MHz clock speed. It consists of 86 I/O pins that can be directly connected to the I/O devices. To reproduce the number of I/O devices of SWaT, we used 32 DI (push-buttons, switches and scripts), 13 AI (temperature and ultrasonic sensors) and 16 DO (light emitter diodes (LEDs)).

PLC program: we have designed a control program written in ladder diagram that has similar complexity to the one in SWaT (a sample diagram is shown on Fig. 3 (in Appendix)). It consists of various types of instructions such as logical (AND, OR, NOT, SR (set-reset latch)), arithmetic (addition (ADD), multiplication (MUL)), comparisons (equal (EQ), greater than (GT), less than (LT), less than or equal (LE)), counters (up-counter (CTU)), timers (turn on timer (TON), turn off timer (TOF)), contacts (normally-open (NO), normally-closed (NC)), and coils (normally-open (NO), normally-closed (NC)). We stated complexity of the program both in terms of number of instructions and lines of code (LOC). The overall PLC program consists of 129 instructions; details are shown on Table 4 (in Appendix). Size of the program (when translated to C code) is 508 LOC.

Communication frequency: the communication architecture of open-SWaT (illustrated on Fig. 1) consists of analogous communicating components with that of SWaT. Open-SWaT uses both type of modbus communication protocols – modbus TCP (for Ethernet or wireless communication) and modbus RTU (for serial communication). The communication among PLCs is via modbus TCP or modbus RTU whereas the communication between PLCs and the SCADA system is via modbus TCP. Frequency of communication among PLCs and the SCADA system

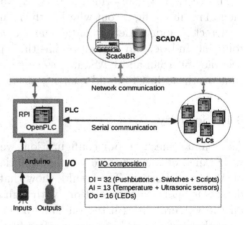

Fig. 1. Architecture of open-SWaT [30]

is similar to that in SWaT. The communication between PLCs and Arduino is via USB serial communication. The frequency of receiving inputs from Arduino or sending outputs to Arduino is 100 Hz.

Real-time constraint: based on the real-time constraint of SWaT, we set 10 ms cycle time (real-time constraint) to each PLC in open-SWaT.

SCADA system: we use ScadaBR [39], a full SCADA system consisting of web-based HMI.

In summary, the design of open-SWaT is expected to be very close to SWaT. In particular, the PLCs (in both cases) are expected to operate similarly. Because their hardware specifications, the inputs they receive from sensors, the PLC program they execute, the control command they issue, the number of nodes they are communicating with, the frequency of communications, and so on, are designed to be similar. Thus, we expect that the MSO in open-SWaT would also remain close to that in SWaT. Therefore, if the MSO is tolerable in open-SWaT, it would be the same for SWaT. In the future, we plan to replace the PLCs at SWaT with the open-source and memory-safety enabled PLCs of open-SWaT.

5.2   Measurement Details

We have implemented a function using POSIX clocks (in nanosecond resolution) that measures execution time of each operation in the PLC scan cycle. The function measures elapsed time of each operation. Results will be then exported to external files for further manipulation, e.g., computing MSO and plotting graphs. We run 50000 scan cycles for each PLC operation to measure the overall performance of the PLC.

6   Evaluation and Discussion of the Results

In this section, we performed a detailed evaluation and discussion of the experimental results to figure out whether the memory-safety tools are accurate enough to detect memory-safety violations and efficient enough to work in a CPS environment. In brief, our evaluation has three parts: *security (accuracy)* – detection accuracy of ASan and KASan, *performance (efficiency)* – tolerability of its runtime overhead in CPS, and *memory usage* overheads.

6.1   Security

As a sanity check on our configuration, we have evaluated our setup against a wide-range of memory-safety vulnerabilities to explore the detection accuracy of ASan and KASan. The results show that, as in the original paper [20], ASan detects memory-safety violations with high accuracy – without false positives for all the vulnerabilities listed on Table 3 (in Appendix) and rare false negatives for global buffer overflow and use-after-free vulnerabilities due to the exceptions discussed on [20].

As discussed on Sect. 2.4, KASan's error coverage is purposely limited to buffer overflows and use-after-free vulnerabilities for performance reason. We evaluated its detection accuracy against these vulnerabilities in the Linux kernel and it accurately detects them; no false positives or negatives were discovered or reported so far. Both tools also effectively mitigate the detected violations regardless of the mitigation limitations discussed on Sect. 4.3.

6.2   Performance

According to published benchmarks [20], the average runtime overhead of ASan is about 73%. However, all measurements were taken on a non-CPS environment. With our full-stack memory-safety enforcement, i.e., ASan + KASan, the average overhead is 94.32%. The overall performance report of the PLC including the execution time of each operation and its respective MSO is depicted on Table 1.

To evaluate tolerability of this overhead, we have checked if it satisfies the conditions defined on Eq. (2) (for average-case) and Eq. (3) (for worst-case). As shown on Table 1, $mean(\hat{T}_s) = 865.10\,\mu s$, and $T_c = 10000\,\mu s$. Therefore, according to Eq. (2), the overhead is tolerable for SWaT with the average-case scenario.

To evaluate the tolerability in the worst-case scenario, we check if it satisfies Eq. (3). As shown on Table 1, $max(\hat{T}_s) = 5238.46\,\mu s$, and $T_c = 10000\,\mu s$. It is still tolerable, thus ASan satisfies the real-time constraint of SWaT both in the average-case and worst-case scenarios. Therefore, we can conclude that SWaT would tolerate the overhead caused by memory-safe compilation, while significantly increasing its security.

Table 1. Memory-safety overheads (MSO)

Operations	Number of cycles	Network devices	CPU speed (in MHz)	T_s (in µs)		$\hat{T}_s$ (in µs)		MSO (mean)	
				Mean	Max	Mean	Max	in µs	in %
Input scan	50000	6	200	114.94	995.10	204.53	1202.28	89.59	77.95
Program execution	50000	6	200	150.32	716.62	305.59	1982.57	155.27	103.29
Output update	50000	6	200	179.93	1020.47	354.98	2053.61	175.05	97.29
Full scan time	50000	6	200	445.19	2732.19	865.10	5238.46	419.91	94.32

6.3   Memory Usage

We also evaluated memory usage overheads of our security measure. Table 2 (in Appendix) summarizes the increase in virtual memory usage, real memory usage, binary size and shared library usage collected by reading VmPeak, VmRSS, VmExe and VmLib fields, respectively, from */proc/self/status*. It shows a huge increase in virtual memory usage (30.45×). This is mainly because of the allocation of large redzones with *malloc*. However, the real memory usage overhead is only 1.40×. These overheads are still acceptable since most PLCs nowadays come with at least 1 GB memory size.

6.4   Validation and Sensitivity Analysis

More generally, how can we evaluate a system's tolerability to overheads? On the one hand, we may perform an empirical analysis such as the one discussed in the previous subsections. But we may also attempt to isolate the individual factors impacting performance on a CPS in order to perform a design-time analysis.

Empirical Analysis. Suppose the tolerability argument is represented by Φ, where Φ represents Eq. (2) (for average-case) and Eq. (3) (for worst-case). We have empirically measured the scan time of each 50000 scan cycles, say $\hat{T}_{s,1}, \ldots, \hat{T}_{s,50000}$. Because of the fact that the bar between the worst-case scan time measured, i.e., $max(\hat{T}_s) = 5238.46\,\mu s$ and the tolerability limit, i.e., $T_c = 10000\,\mu s$ is still 47.62%, we can fairly conclude that the probability of getting $\hat{T}_s{}'$ such that $\hat{T}_s{}' \not\models \Phi$ is very rare. Therefore, the empirical analysis can be used as one way of validating tolerability of the MSO even though it cannot prove *completeness* of the argument. However, a more thorough analysis is needed to conclude that there are no corner cases that might suddenly occur and cause more significant delays.

WCST Analysis. Thus, a deeper analysis to validate the tolerability argument is needed. This is a theoretical analysis (beyond the empirical results) to show that there would not occur a new WCST $\hat{T}_s{}'$ such that $\hat{T}_s{}' > T_c$. For simplicity, let us refer the occurrence of the condition $\hat{T}_s{}' > T_c$ as an *intolerability* condition. For this analysis, first we experimentally identified the main factors that can have significant effect on the PLC scan time and MSO. We discussed below how the factors can affect the scan time and why they would not lead to the *intolerability* condition.

- **CPU speed** $(S_{CPU} \in \mathbb{R})$: obviously, clock speed of the processor is a major factor for the PLC performance. It determines how much clock cycles the CPU performs per second, hence it determines how much instructions the PLC can process per second. S_{CPU} affects all operations of the PLC. However, since S_{CPU} is fixed with "userspace" governor, it would not lead to *intolerability*.
- **Memory size** $(S_M \in \mathbb{R})$: size of memory is fixed. The memory size needed for memory mapping and redzones allocation (due to the memory-safe compilation) is already allocated at compile-time. Cache memory size is not also a big issue in CPS. Because CPS data such as sensor data, control commands and state information get updated very frequently. Thus, data caching is not that much relevant in CPS. Therefore, S_M would not lead to *intolerability*.
- **Number of sensors** $(N_S \in \mathbb{N})$: the number of input devices (sensors) connected to the PLC is one factor that significantly affect the PLC scan time and MSO. Because, the time to scan inputs depends on the number of sensors connected with the PLC. However, N_S is fixed, hence it would not cause the *intolerability* condition to happen.
- **Number of actuators** $(N_A \in \mathbb{N})$: the number of output devices (actuators) connected to the PLC is also another factor that has significant effect on the PLC scan time and MSO. Because, the time to update outputs depends on the number of output devices connected with the PLC. However, since N_A is fixed, it would not lead to *intolerability*.
- **Complexity of the PLC program** $(C_P \in \mathbb{R}^Z)$: As discussed on Sect. 5.1, the PLC program can consist of various types of instructions. Each instruction has its own execution time. Therefore, C_P can be expressed in terms of

the number and type of instructions that the overall program consists of ($Z = $ {number of instructions, type of instructions}). As such, it is a major factor for the PLC scan time as it affects the control program execution time. However, C_P is fixed and the program does not also contain loops or recursion functions. Thus, it would not lead to the *intolerability* condition.

- *Communication frequency* ($C_F \in \mathbb{R}$): the PLC communicates with various devices such as RIO (sensors and actuators), other PLCs and SCADA systems. The communication frequency can be expressed in terms of the number of packets the PLC sends or receives to/from other communicating devices. Handling all such communications can take significant amount of time. In particular, it significantly affects the PLC's performance when the PLC handles the concurrency issues between the scan cycle and communication threads to access shared resources, such as shared buffers [30]. Therefore, the communication frequency between the PLC and other communicating entities is another factor for the PLC scan time. However, when the PLC communicates with n nodes, it receives or sends packets with a constant rate. Thus, the C_F is fixed. In addition, realistic PLCs (as real-time systems) efficiently handle concurrency problems. Therefore, the C_F would not result the *intolerability* condition.

We also performed a sensitivity analysis on the factors in regard to its effect on the PLC scan time and MSO. This analysis will help us to extrapolate mathematical formulas predicting the expected MSO and its tolerability to a given CPS. A detailed account of our sensitivity analysis is provided in our previous work [30].

7   Related Work

In this section, we explore related works done in providing memory-safety solutions against memory-safety attacks and measuring and analyzing memory-safety overheads in the CPS environment.

In our earlier work [30], we enforced ASan to a CPS environment and measured its runtime overhead (81.82%). However, it was only a user-space enforcement and the critical kernel-level security concern was ignored. To address that limitation, we enforced a full-stack memory-safety, i.e., ASan + KASan, in our current work. With a similar setup but a different kernel configuration, the average overhead of the proposed solution is 94.32%. Meaning, it incurs an additional overhead of 12.5%, but with a significant boost in security. To enhance comprehensiveness of our experimental results, we also increased the number of scan cycles (whose scan time is empirically measured) from 10000 to 50000.

SoftBoundCETS is a compile-time code-instrumentation tool that detects all violations of spatial memory-safety (SoftBound [21]) and temporal memory-safety (CETS [22]) in C. It is a complete memory-safety tool that works under the LLVM environment. However, its runtime overhead is very high (116%) as compare to ASan (73%). In addition, it is incompatible for the CPS environment; because it is implemented only for the x86-64 target architecture and it is also dependent on the LLVM infrastructure.

Cooprider et al. [40] enforced efficient memory-safety solution for TinyOS applications by integrating Deputy [41], an annotation based type and memory-safety compiler, with nesC [42], a C compiler. Thus, they managed to detect memory-safety violations with high accuracy. To make this memory-safety solution practical in terms of CPU and memory usage, they did aggressive optimization by implementing a static analyzer and optimizer tool, called cXprop. With cXprop, they managed to reduce memory-safety overhead of Deputy from 24% to 5.2%, and they also improved memory usage through dead code elimination. However, their solution has limitations to apply it in a CPS environment, because it is dependent on runtime libraries of TinyOS.

Zhang et al. [43] modeled the trade-off between privacy and performance in CPS. While he leveraged the differential privacy approach to preserve privacy of CPS, he also analyzed and modeled its performance overhead. He proposed an approach that optimizes the system performance while preserving privacy of CPS. This work is interesting from point of view of analyzing performance overheads in CPS, but it is not from memory-safety perspective.

Stefanov et al. [44] proposed a new model and platform for the SCADA system of an integrated CPS. With the proposed platform, he modeled real-time supervision of CPS, performance of CPS based on communication latencies, and also he assessed and modeled communication and cyber security of the SCADA system. He followed a generic approach to assess and control various aspects of the CPS. However, he did not specifically work on memory-safety attacks or memory-safety overheads. Vuong et al. [45] tried to evaluate performance overhead of a cyber-physical intrusion detection technique. But, it was not on memory-safety either.

Several CFI based solutions (e.g., [18,19]) have been also developed against memory-safety attacks. However, CFI based solutions have some limitations in general (i) determining the required control flow graph (often using static analysis) is hard and requires a significant amount of memory; (ii) attacks that do not divert control flow of the program cannot be detected (for instance using Data Oriented attacks [46]). These and other reasons can limit the applicability of CFI solutions in the CPS environment.

In summary, to the best of our knowledge, there is no prior research work that enforced a full-stack memory-safety solution specifically to the CPS environment, and that measured and evaluated tolerability of the induced memory-safety overhead in accordance to the real-time constraints of cyber-physical systems.

8   Conclusion

In this work, we presented the results of implementing a strong full-stack memory-safety enforcement in a simulated albeit realistic industrial control system using ASan and KASan. Our setup allowed us to benchmark and empirically measure the runtime overhead of the enforcement and, based on the real-time constraints of an ICS, to judge the applicability in a realistic scenario. Our experiments show that the real-time constraints of SWaT can be largely met even when implementing a strong memory-safety countermeasure in realistic hardware. We also preliminary discuss what factors impact the performance of such a system, in a first attempt to generalize our results.

In the future, we intend to study other CPS with different constraints, e.g., in power grid and urban transportation systems. Such studies will allow us to extrapolate formulas predicting the tolerability of systems to MSO and thus aiding in the design of resilient CPS before such systems are deployed.

Appendix

Table 2. Memory usage overheads (in MB)

Category	Original	Instrumented	Increase
Virtual memory usage	20.412	621.580	30.45×
Real memory usage	8.172	11.476	1.40×
Binary size	0.138	0.316	2.29×
Shared library usage	2.832	4.300	1.52×

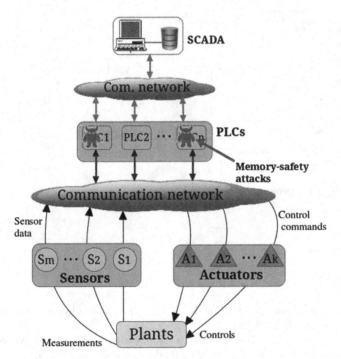

Fig. 2. The CPS architecture and memory-safety attacks [30]

Table 3. Detection accuracy of ASan

Vulnerabilities	False positive	False negative
Stack buffer overflow	No	No
Heap buffer overflow	No	No
Global buffer overflow	No	Rare
Dangling pointers	No	Rare
Use-after-return	No	No
Initialization order bugs	No	No
Memory leaks	No	No

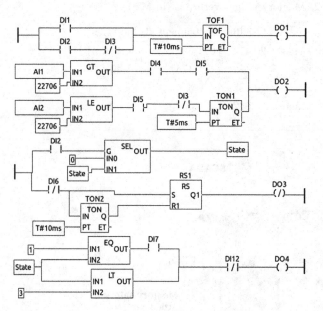

Fig. 3. Sample PLC program in ladder diagram [30]

Table 4. Instruction count

Instructions	Count
Logical	
AND	17
OR	14
NOT	5
SR	1
Arithmetic	
ADD	1
MUL	2
Comparisons	
EQ	3
GT	3
LT	2
LE	2
Timers	
TON	3
TOF	9
Counters	
CTU	1
Selections	
SEL	1
MAX	1
Contacts	
NO	38
NC	3
Coils	
NO	21
NC	2
Total	129

References

1. Sha, L., Gopalakrishnan, S., Liu, X., Wang, Q.: Cyber-physical systems: a new frontier. In: SUTC 2008 (2008)
2. Lee, E.A., Seshia, S.A.: Introduction to Embedded Systems - A Cyber-Physical Systems Approach, 2nd edn, version 2.0 edn. LeeSeshia.org (2015)
3. Lee, E.A.: Cyber physical systems: design challenges. In: ISORC 2008 (2008)
4. MITRE: Common Vulnerabilities and Exposures. https://cve.mitre.org/
5. CVE-5814. https://cve.mitre.org/cgi-bin/cvename.cgi?name=CVE-2016-5814

6. CVE-6438. https://cve.mitre.org/cgi-bin/cvename.cgi?name=CVE-2012-6438
7. CVE-6436. https://cve.mitre.org/cgi-bin/cvename.cgi?name=CVE-2012-6436
8. CVE-0674. https://cve.mitre.org/cgi-bin/cvename.cgi?name=CVE-2013-0674
9. CVE-1449. https://cve.mitre.org/cgi-bin/cvename.cgi?name=CVE-2015-1449
10. CVE-0929. https://cve.mitre.org/cgi-bin/cvename.cgi?name=CVE-2012-0929
11. CVE-7937. https://cve.mitre.org/cgi-bin/cvename.cgi?name=CVE-2015-7937
12. CVE-5007. https://cve.mitre.org/cgi-bin/cvename.cgi?name=CVE-2011-5007
13. NVD: NVD Statistics on The Linux Kernel Vulnerabilities (2018). https://nvd.nist.gov/vuln/search/results?adv_search=false&form_type=basic&results_type=overview&search_type=all&query=linux+kernel
14. Berger, E.D., Zorn, B.G.: DieHard: probabilistic memory safety for unsafe languages. In: PLDI 2006 (2006)
15. Novark, G., Berger, E.D.: DieHarder: securing the heap. In: CCS 2010 (2010)
16. Kharbutli, M., Jiang, X., Solihin, Y., Venkataramani, G., Prvulovic, M.: Comprehensively and efficiently protecting the heap. In: ASPLOS 2006 (2006)
17. Abadi, M., Budiu, M., Erlingsson, U., Ligatti, J.: Control-flow integrity. In: CCS 2005, pp. 340–353 (2005)
18. Zhang, M., Sekar, R.: Control flow integrity for cots binaries. In: USENIX 2013
19. Tice, C., Roeder, T., Collingbourne, P., Checkoway, S., Erlingsson, Ú., Lozano, L., Pike, G.: Enforcing forward-edge control-flow integrity in GCC & LLVM. In: USENIX 2014, pp. 941–955 (2014)
20. Serebryany, K., Bruening, D., Potapenko, A., Vyukov, D.: AddressSanitizer: a fast address sanity checker. In: USENIX ATC 2012 (2012)
21. Nagarakatte, S., Zhao, J., Martin, M.M., Zdancewic, S.: SoftBound: highly compatible and complete spatial memory safety for C. In: PLDI 2009 (2009)
22. Nagarakate, S., Zhao, J., Martin, M.M., Zdancewic, S.: CETS: compiler enforced temporal safety for C. In: ISMM 2010 (2010)
23. Simpson, M.S., Barua, R.K.: MemSafe: ensuring the spatial and temporal memory safety of C at runtime. Softw.: Pract. Exp. **43**(1), 93–128 (2013)
24. Bruening, D., Zhao, Q.: Practical memory checking with Dr. Memory. In: CGO 2011 (2011)
25. Necula, G.C., Condit, J., Harren, M., McPeak, S., Weimer, W.: CCured: type-safe retrofitting of legacy software. ACM Trans. Progr. Lang. Syst. **27**(3), 477–526 (2005)
26. Eigler, F.C.: Mudflap: Pointer Use Checking for C/C++. In: GCC Developer's Summit. Red Hat Inc (2003)
27. KASAN: The Kernel Address Sanitizer (2018). https://www.kernel.org/doc/html/v4.12/dev-tools/kasan.html
28. iTrust: Secure Water Treatment (SWaT) Testbed. https://itrust.sutd.edu.sg/research/testbeds/secure-water-treatment-swat/
29. Ahmed, C.M., Adepu, S., Mathur, A.: Limitations of state estimation based cyber attack detection schemes in industrial control systems. In: SCSP-W 2016 (2016)
30. Chekole, E.G., Castellanos, J.H., Ochoa, M., Yau, D.K.Y.: Enforcing memory safety in cyber-physical systems. In: Katsikas, S., et al. (eds.) SECPRE 2017, CyberICPS 2017. LNCS, vol. 10683, pp. 127–144. Springer, Cham (2017). https://doi.org/10.1007/978-3-319-72817-9_9
31. AddressSanitizer Github Repository. https://github.com/google/sanitizers/wiki/AddressSanitizerComparisonOfMemoryTools
32. KASAN Wiki: The Kernel Address Sanitizer Wiki (2018). https://github.com/google/kasan/wiki

33. KASAN Bug Report: List of Kernel Bugs Detected by KASan (2018). https://github.com/google/kasan/wiki/Found-Bugs
34. TOFINO SECURITY. https://www.tofinosecurity.com/blog/plc-security-risk-controller-operating-systems/
35. LinPAC. http://www.icpdas.com/root/product/solutions/pac/linpac/linpac-8000_introduction.html/
36. OpenPLC. http://www.openplcproject.com/
37. WAGO: Linux Programmable Fieldbus Controller
38. CERT.ORG: Vulnerability Notes Database
39. ScadaBR. http://www.scadabr.com.br/
40. Cooprider, N., Archer, W., Eide, E., Gay, D., Regehr, J.: Efficient memory safety for TinyOS. In: SenSys 2007, pp. 205–218 (2007)
41. The Deputy Project (2007). http://deputy.cs.berkeley.edu
42. Gay, D., Levis, P., von Behren, R., Welsh, M., Brewer, E., Culler, D.: The nesC language: a holistic approach to networked embedded systems. In: PLDI 2003 (2003)
43. Zhang, H., Shu, Y., Cheng, P., Chen, J.: Privacy and performance trade-off in cyber-physical systems. IEEE Netw. **30**(2), 62–66 (2016)
44. Stefanov, A., Liu, C.C., Govindarasu, M., Wu, S.S.: SCADA modeling for performance and vulnerability assessment of integrated cyber-physical systems. Intern. Trans. Electr. Energy Syst. **25**(3), 498–519 (2015)
45. Vuong, T.P., Loukas, G., Gan, D.: Performance evaluation of cyber-physical intrusion detection on a robotic vehicle. In: IEEE International Conference On Computer and Information Technology; Ubiquitous Computing and Communications; Dependable, Autonomic and Secure Computing; Pervasive Intelligence and Computing (2015)
46. Hu, H., Shinde, S., Adrian, S., Chua, Z.L., Saxena, P., Liang, Z.: Data-oriented programming: on the expressiveness of non-control data attacks. In: SP 2016 (2016)

Model Checking the Information Flow Security of Real-Time Systems

Christopher Gerking[1]($\boxtimes$), David Schubert[2], and Eric Bodden[1,2]

[1] Heinz Nixdorf Institute, Paderborn University,
Paderborn, Germany
christopher.gerking@upb.de
[2] Fraunhofer IEM, Paderborn, Germany

Abstract. Cyber-physical systems are processing large amounts of sensitive information, but are increasingly often becoming the target of cyber attacks. Thus, it is essential to verify the absence of unauthorized information flow at design time before the systems get deployed. Our paper addresses this problem by proposing a novel approach to model-check the information flow security of cyber-physical systems represented by timed automata. We describe the transformation into so-called *test automata*, reducing the verification to a reachability test that is carried out using the off-the-shelf model checker UPPAAL. Opposed to related work, we analyze the real-time behavior of systems, allowing software engineers to precisely identify timing channels that would enable attackers to draw conclusions from the system's response times. We illustrate the approach by detecting a timing channel in a simplified model of a cyber-manufacturing system.

Keywords: Model checking · Information flow · Security · Real time

1 Introduction

Cyber-physical systems [35] are entrusted a fast-growing amount of sensitive data, but are inherently vulnerable to security breaches such as manipulation or leakage of information [15,25]. One subtle attack vector are *timing channels* [11], allowing attackers to infer sensitive information by observing the system's response times. In the worst case, such hidden flows of information could even be exploited to manipulate the physical behavior and compromise the safety of systems. Thus, to make cyber-physical systems secure by design [39], it is essential to verify their *information flow security* before they get deployed.

Model-driven engineering is a widely used approach to securing cyber-physical systems [38], making the software under development accessible to formal verification. A well-established formal definition of information flow security

---

The stamp on the top of this paper refers to an approval process conducted by the ESSoS Artifact Evaluation Committee.

© Springer International Publishing AG, part of Springer Nature 2018
M. Payer et al. (Eds.): ESSoS 2018, LNCS 10953, pp. 27–43, 2018.
https://doi.org/10.1007/978-3-319-94496-8_3

is *noninterference* [26] which requires that the observable behavior of systems must not depend on secrets. A well-known verification approach for noninterference is *bisimulation*, checking that a system exhibits the same observable behavior as a restricted variant of itself that is known to be secure by definition [19].

Nevertheless, checking the information flow security of cyber-physical systems is a challenging problem for software engineers because they are faced with *real-time systems*, restricted by hard real-time constraints imposed by their physical environment [12]. Therefore, models of cyber-physical systems are based on formalisms like *timed automata* [5], and the real-time behavior of these models needs to be taken into account during verification to detect leaks like timing channels. Verification techniques such as model checking of timed automata are available [4], but involve sophisticated tools that are hard to implement from scratch. In this paper, we therefore address the problem of applying off-the-shelf verification tools to check the information flow security of real-time systems.

Bisimulation of real-time systems is known to be decidable by existing verification techniques [14]. Nevertheless, previous approaches towards applied verification of information flow security have not taken into account real-time behavior [3,17,20,32]. Therefore, they fail to detect leaks such as timing channels precisely. Related work on the information flow security of timed automata exists [6,8,13,34,45], but has spent little effort on how to apply tool-supported model checking techniques in practice. Thus, in summary, none of the previous approaches fully combines real-time behavior with applied model checking.

In this paper, we fill in these gaps by reducing the check for noninterference of timed automata to a *refinement* check, adapting the work by Heinzemann et al. [30] to the application field of information flow security. This check is based on model transformations to construct a *test automaton* [1], introducing a dedicated location that is only reachable when violating a bisimulation between the original automaton and a secure-by-definition variant of itself. By model checking the reachability of these dedicated locations using the off-the-shelf tool UPPAAL [9], we obtain a novel verification technique for the information flow security of real-time systems. In contrast to related approaches, our work is based on timed automata, taking into account the real-time behavior of cyber-physical systems. Unlike other related work, we focus on applied model checking to meet the needs of software engineering practitioners.

We illustrate the approach using a simplified model of a cyber-manufacturing system that interacts with a cloud-based service market. The system must not allow market participants to draw any conclusions about business secrets.

In summary, this paper makes the following contributions:

- We propose a model transformation process, reducing the check for information flow security of real-time systems to a model checking problem.

- At the core of this process, we illustrate the construction of test automata to check noninterference of timed automata.
- We give a proof of concept by detecting a timing channel in a simplified model of a cyber-manufacturing system.

Paper Organization: We introduce fundamentals in Sect. 2, and discuss related work in Sect. 3. In Sect. 4, we describe our approach of checking information flow security of real-time systems. We give a proof of concept in Sect. 5, before concluding in Sect. 6.

2   Fundamentals

In this section, we recall timed automata (cf. Sect. 2.1), timed bisimulation (cf. Sect. 2.2), and noninterference (cf. Sect. 2.3). Based on these fundamental concepts, we introduce our motivating example in Sect. 2.4.

2.1   Timed Automata

The formalism of *timed automata* [5] is used to model real-time behavior of stateful systems. A timed automaton is essentially a directed graph containing a finite set of locations, connected by a finite set of labeled edges. We use the definition of timed automata by Bengtsson and Yi [10]. Timed automata extend finite automata by real-valued variables that represent *clocks*. Clocks are initialized with zero, increase at the same rate, and may be set back to zero by using *resets* that can be assigned to edges.

Clock constraints restrict the behavior of an automaton with respect to the valuation of its clocks. A clock constraint is a conjunction of atomic constraints of the form $x \sim n$ or $x - y \sim n$, where x and y are clocks, $n \in \mathbb{N}$, and $\sim \in \{\le, <, =, >, \ge\}$ [10]. Clock constraints are used as *invariants* and *time guards*. Invariants are assigned to locations. An active location is forced to be left by firing an edge before the location's invariant expires. Therefore, invariants have to be downward closed, i.e., only $\le$ and $<$ operators are permitted. Time guards are assigned to edges. An edge may fire (i.e., it is *enabled*) only if its time guard evaluates to true. In addition, edges are labeled with actions, whereas firing an edge represents the execution of the action its is labeled with. To represent edges without an action, we refer to τ as the empty action.

Assuming a set $\mathcal{C}$ of clocks, a set $\mathcal{B}(\mathcal{C})$ of clock constraints, and an alphabet Σ of actions, the syntax of a timed automaton is defined as follows [10]:

Definition 1. *A timed automaton A is a tuple $\langle L, l_0, E, I \rangle$ where*

- *L is a finite set of locations,*
- *$l_0 \in L$ is the initial location,*
- *$E \subseteq L \times \mathcal{B}(\mathcal{C}) \times \Sigma \times 2^{\mathcal{C}} \times L$ is the set of edges where $\rho \in \mathcal{B}(\mathcal{C})$ is the time guard, $\mu \in \Sigma$ is the action, and $\lambda \in 2^{\mathcal{C}}$ is the set of clock resets,*
- *$I : L \to \mathcal{B}(\mathcal{C})$ assigns invariants to locations.*

UPPAAL[1] [9] is an off-the-shelf model checker for timed automata that is commonly applied by software engineering practitioners, and frequently integrated into domain-specific verification tools [43]. In the scope of this paper, we apply UPPAAL to verify the information flow security of timed automata.

2.2   Timed Bisimulation

Bisimulation is a notion of observational equivalence that requires the observable behavior of two systems to be indistinguishable. *Timed bisimulation* is an extension of bisimulation for real-time systems which is known to be decidable [14]. Intuitively, two systems are equivalent in terms of timed bisimulation if they execute the same sequences of observable actions in the same time intervals. We refer the reader to [10] for a formal definition in the context of timed automata.

There are two variants of timed bisimulation. *Strong* timed bisimulation is more restrictive as it considers all actions of a system as being observable, including τ actions. In the context of our paper, this assumption is too strong because we consider τ actions as internal and, therefore, not observable. In contrast to this, *weak* timed bisimulation ignores the execution of internal τ actions [14]. In the following, we consider only this weak variant of timed bisimulation between two timed automata A and B (denoted by $A \approx B$), and refer to it as timed bisimulation for brevity.

2.3   Noninterference

Noninterference was introduced by Goguen and Meseguer [26] to define information flow security of deterministic finite automata, such that the publicly observable behavior must not depend on sensitive information. If so, public observations never enable an unprivileged actor to distinguish whether or not sensitive information was processed. In particular, no conclusions are possible about *which* sensitive information was actually received. To characterize the sensitivity of information, noninterference is based on a separation between sensitive (or *high*) actions Σ_H and public (or *low*) actions Σ_L with $\Sigma_H, \Sigma_L \subseteq \Sigma$.

For nondeterministic systems such as timed automata, noninterference is frequently defined on the basis of bisimulation [19,34,45]. Noninterference holds if the publicly observable behavior of a system cannot be distinguished from a restricted behavior that is secure by definition. To define this property more precisely, we distinguish between *input actions* received from the environment, and *output actions* sent to the environment. Based on this distinction, noninterference reduces to a bisimulation of the publicly observable behavior between

1. the original system, and
2. a secure-by-definition system with all sensitive input actions *disabled*.

---

[1] http://uppaal.org

Disabling sensitive input actions ensures that the secure-by-definition system behaves as if no sensitive information is ever processed. By disabling only input actions, we assume that all sensitive information is received from the environment, and never generated internally without depending on sensitive inputs [29].

To identify deviations only in the publicly observable behavior, non-public actions need to be *hidden* from the bisimulation, i.e., treated as non-observable. In the following definition, $\backslash_I$ denotes the disabling of inputs, and / the hiding of actions, whereas $\Sigma_{\bar{L}} = \Sigma \setminus \Sigma_L$ is the set of non-public actions.

Definition 2. *Timed noninterference holds for a timed automaton A, if and only if $A \mathbin{/} \Sigma_{\bar{L}} \approx (A \setminus_I \Sigma_H) \mathbin{/} \Sigma_{\bar{L}}$.*

2.4 Motivating Example

In our approach, we assume timed automata to be embedded in component-based software architectures, which are commonly used for the software design of cyber-physical systems [16]. In Fig. 1, we show a software component named ManufacturingSystem as a model of our example announced in Sect. 1. The component embeds a timed automaton that drives the application-level communication between the system and its environment. The communication is carried out by means of asynchronous message passing, whereas the set of messages corresponds to the alphabet Σ. Accordingly, when messages are received, they are buffered until they are processed by an input action of the automaton. Asynchronous communication is a characteristic property of cyber-physical systems because they are often spatially divided and dynamically interconnected over wireless networks. In Fig. 1, we use / to separate input from output actions.

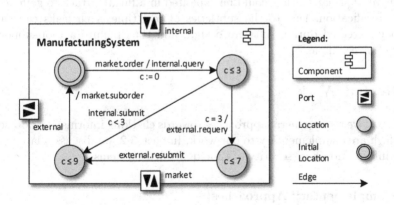

Fig. 1. Example timed automaton of a cyber-manufacturing system

Our example component uses three ports to pass messages. The market port is used to interact with the service market. Whenever a production order is received from the market, the internal port is the preferred way to access the product specification, provided that it is available as an in-house resource. Alternatively, access to the specification may also be purchased from a business partner over the external port. The messages passed over the market port are public (represented by the set Σ_L), whereas the messages passed over the internal port are sensitive (represented by Σ_H). In our example, messages passed over the external port are not further characterized as public or sensitive because information flow needs to be detected only from the internal to the market port.

In the following, we describe the behavior of the automaton from Fig. 1. Whenever the automaton is in its initial location and receives an order message from the market, it sends a query for the product specification over the internal port. At the same time, it sets the clock c to zero which acts as a timeout. If the internal port does not provide the specification in terms of a submit message within three time units (i.e., the company does not possess the specification), a requery message is sent over the external port to purchase the specification from a business partner. In this case, the example system assumes that the specification is provided in terms of a resubmit message within four further time units ($c \leq 7$), i.e., a deadlock caused by an overdue message can never occur. Finally, if the specification is delivered from either the internal or external port, the system orders the corresponding subproducts from the market by sending a suborder message in the time interval $c \leq 9$.

However, the system violates timed noninterference because the effective timing of the public suborder message depends on whether or not the specification is possessed by the company. If possessed, the specification is provided by the sensitive internal port, and suborder may be sent when $c < 3$. Otherwise, when provided by the external port, the suborder message can only be sent when $c \geq 3$. This deviation represents a timing channel that allows market participants to infer whether the company possesses the product specification or not. This knowledge is sensitive information that could be exploited in a future attack to gain access to the specification. Due to the subtleties of real time, such leaks can easily remain undetected during software design, and thus require a tool-supported verification technique.

3   Related Work

In Sect. 3.1, we recall general approaches towards checking information flow security, which are complementary to our work. In Sect. 3.2, we discuss related work on the information flow security of time-dependent systems.

3.1   Complementary Approaches

Unwinding [27] is a traditional verification technique to infer global information flow security from local properties of individual system actions (e.g., state transitions). In the context of real-time systems, this approach is hindered by the infinite, real-valued state space which makes such local properties hard to identify. *Language-based security* [42] is concerned with secure information flow at the level of programming languages, thus using a different model of computation compared to our automata-based approach. In this area, *type systems* are often used to enforce information flow security of programs statically. Furthermore, a technique called *self-composition* has been proposed [7], reducing language-based security to a logical formulation that is amenable to automated verification, similar to our approach in the context of automata-based systems. We refer the reader to [21,37] for a comparison of information flow security under different models of computation. Another complementary approach is the one by Finkbeiner et al. on model checking *hyperproperties* [18]. Unlike standard *safety* or *liveness* properties, hyperproperties relate different executions of a system. Thereby, they cover information flow security properties like noninterference. Whereas hyperproperties involve a novel theory of specification and verification, our focus is on applied verification using off-the-shelf tools.

3.2 Time-Dependent Information Flow Security

In Table 1, we compare related work on the information flow security of time-dependent systems against the core characteristics of our approach, which combines dense real-time behavior with applied verification. Furthermore, we build on automata as the underlying model of computation, which are commonly used as a natural, well-established modeling approach [36]. Finally, according to our example given in Sect. 2.4, we focus on application-level modeling, i.e., we abstract from responsibilities like scheduling.

Table 1. Comparison of related works on time-dependent information flow security

	Dense real-time	Automata-based	Application level	Applied verification
Evans and Schneider [17]	✗	✗	✓	✓
Focardi et al. [20]	✗	✗	✓	✓
Akella et al. [3]	✗	✗	✓	✓
Agat [2]	✗	✗	✓	✗
Giacobazzi and Mastroeni [24]	✗	✗	✓	✗
Rafnsson et al. [40]	✗	✗	✓	✗
Köpf and Basin [32]	✗	✓	✗	✓
Roscoe and Huang [41]	✓	✗	✓	✗
Son and Alves-Foss [44]	✓	✗	✗	✗
Kashyap et al. [31]	✓	✗	✗	✗
Cassez [13]	✓	✓	✓	✗
Lanotte et al. [34]	✓	✓	✓	✗
Benattar et al. [8]	✓	✓	✓	✗
Vasilikos et al. [45]	✓	✓	✓	✗
Barbuti and Tesei [6]	✓	✓	✓	(✓)
This paper	✓	✓	✓	✓

The works by Evans and Schneider [17], Focardi et al. [20], and Akella et al. [3] analyse the security of process algebras. Existing verification techniques like theorem proving [17] or partial model checking [20] are applied, even in the context of cyber-physical systems [3]. By using process algebra, the authors differ from our automata-based approach in terms of their model of computation. In the context of language-based security, the work by Agat [2], Giaccobazzi and Mastroeni [24], as well as Rafnsson et al. [40] uses imperative programs as yet another model of computation. In contrast, the work by Köpf and Basin [32] on synchronous systems is automata-based and also amenable to applied verification. However, all of the above approaches are limited to discrete time, which is insufficient to capture the real-time behavior of cyber-physical systems.

In contrast, other existing approaches consider dense real-time behavior. Roscoe and Huang [41] use process algebra and thereby differ from our automata-based approach. Son and Alves-Foss [44] as well as Kashyap et al. [31] both focus on scheduling of real-time tasks, i.e., do not address the application level.

In the context of timed automata, Cassez [13] presents a real-time security property called *timed opacity* as a generalization of noninterference. The author proves the undecidability of the verification problem, i.e., is not concerned with applied verification. Lanotte et al. [33] consider real-time privacy properties of timed automata, and reduce the verification of such properties to a reachability analysis [28], similar to this paper. In [34], the same authors consider noninterference of timed automata extended by probabilistic behavior. However, the application of existing model checking techniques is beyond the scope of their approach. Benattar et al. [8] enable the synthesis of controllers that ensure noninterference of timed automata. According to this constructive approach, they do not consider applied verification as well. Vasilikos et al. [45] address the security of timed automata that leak some information intentionally. The authors propose an algorithm to impose local security constraints on the elements of an automaton, however, do not enable applied verification using off-the-shelf tools.

Barbuti and Tesei [6] verify noninterference of timed automata. Similar to our approach, they reduce the verification to a reachability analysis using applied model checking. However, their approach only checks that sensitive information does not influence the reachability of locations. This approximation gives rise to both *false positive* and *false negative* errors, and thus is not capable to provide any security guarantee. Nevertheless, the approach by Barbuti and Tesei [6] is the only one that resembles the core characteristics of our paper (cf. Table 1).

4   Checking Noninterference of Timed Automata

In the following, we describe our approach of checking the information flow security of real-time systems. In Sect. 4.1, we give an overview on our approach, and describe the construction of the underlying test automata in Sect. 4.2.

4.1   Refinement Checking

We reduce the verification of timed noninterference to a refinement check for real-time systems as proposed by Heinzemann et al. [30]. The aforementioned work allows to verify refinement relations between real-time systems to check that an abstract behavior is correctly refined by a concrete behavior. The authors reduce the verification to a reachability test [1] that is carried out using model checking techniques. One possible refinement definition is timed bisimulation, as also used to define timed noninterference (cf. Definition 2). Thus, in this paper, we adopt the notion of refinement to check timed noninterference. In Fig. 2, we give an overview on our approach as an extension of the work by Heinzemann et al. [30].

In step ①, we transform a timed automaton A, as described in Sect. 2.4, into an auxiliary automaton A_{sec} that is secure by definition because sensitive inputs are disabled. This restriction corresponds to the automaton $A \setminus_I \Sigma_H$ from Definition 2. We disable sensitive inputs by removing the corresponding edges from A. In the context of the motivating example, Fig. 3a depicts the removal of the edge that processes the submit input over the sensitive internal port.

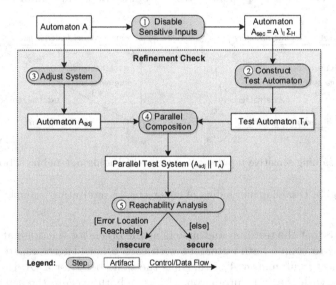

Fig. 2. Reduction of the noninterference check to a refinement check [30]

The resulting automaton A_{sec} enables us to execute a specialized version of the refinement check for timed bisimulation, as proposed by Heinzemann et al. [30]. Thereby, we detect cases where a timed bisimulation between the original automaton A and the secure-by-definition automaton A_{sec} is violated because A deviates from the publicly observable behavior of A_{sec}. At the core of the approach is a *test automaton* [1] that acts as an oracle for the information flow security of the original automaton. In particular, the test automaton detects cases in which the behavior of the original automaton violates timed noninterference. To this end, step ② transforms the automaton A_{sec} into a test automaton T_A, introducing a dedicated *error* location that is reachable when violating timed noninterference by deviating from the secure-by-definition behavior.

As a challenge for the construction of the test automaton, we need to hide all non-public actions from the bisimulation (cf. Definition 2) because only deviations in the public behavior are violations of timed noninterference. In Fig. 3b, we depict those actions that need to be hidden. A natural approach to hide an action is to remove it from the corresponding edge [6, 34], i.e., to replace it by a τ action. However, removing input actions may lead to an increased nondeterminism. The reason is that this approach potentially produces multiple τ transitions that are all executable on the same condition because they are no longer distinguishable by their input actions. However, the refinement check proposed by Heinzemann et al. is restricted to systems with a deterministic transition function [30], i.e., at most one edge can fire on a certain condition. Therefore, in contrast to the default test automata for timed bisimulation [30], our test automata must take responsibility for hiding non-public actions. We describe the construction of these specialized test automata in the upcoming Sect. 4.2.

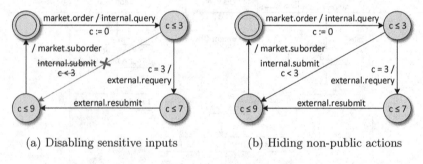

(a) Disabling sensitive inputs   (b) Hiding non-public actions

Fig. 3. Disabling and hiding of actions in the motivating example

To ensure that the test automaton acts as the oracle for the original automaton, we need to couple both automata with each other. Therefore, step ③ creates an adjusted automaton A_{adj} that has the same behavior as A. However, it synchronizes with the test automaton whenever both execute the same action. Furthermore, A_{adj} supports the hiding of non-public actions in the same fashion as the test automaton. In step ④, we compose both T_A and A_{adj} in parallel to enable synchronized execution of the automata. In the final step ⑤, the check for timed noninterference reduces to analyzing the resulting parallel test system for reachability of the *error* location. This reachability test [1] is carried out by means of the UPPAAL model checker, using its parallel composition operator $\|$ to enable the synchronizations between both automata [10]. In the end, the automaton A is secure in terms of timed noninterference, if and only if the *error* location is unreachable on all execution paths.

4.2   Test Automata Construction

To generate test automata, we adjust the construction schema for timed bisimulation proposed by Heinzemann et al. [30] such that it hides non-public communication, as demanded by Definition 2. We adopt the notion of a dedicated *error* location (named *Err* in our case) that is reachable if and only if timed noninterference is violated. Figure 4 illustrates our construction schema including the *Err* location. We apply this schema for each edge $S \rightarrow S'$ of A_{sec}. Our construction must ensure that T_A will ❶ accept secure communication (allowed by A_{sec} and correctly present in the original automaton A), ❷ reject insecure communication (i.e., public communication that is not allowed by A_{sec} but incorrectly present in A), and ❸ detect the absence of communication (i.e., public communication that is allowed by A_{sec} but incorrectly absent in A). Before going into details about the three cases, we introduce additional notation used in Fig. 4. Synchronous input and output actions are denoted by μ? and μ! respectively. The set $\Theta(S)$ includes all actions that are *allowed* in a location S, i.e., all actions of outgoing edges of S. The invariant of S is denoted by $I(S)$. In accordance with Definition 1, ρ is a time guard, and λ is a set of clock resets.

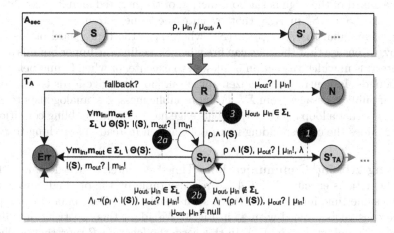

Fig. 4. Construction schema for test automata

Accepting Secure Communication. The edge labeled with ❶ in Fig. 4 ensures that secure communication is accepted by T_A. For each edge $S \rightarrow S'$ in A_{sec}, we add an edge $S_{TA} \rightarrow S'_{TA}$ to T_A. Asynchronous actions of $S \rightarrow S'$ are transformed into synchronous actions to enable synchronization with A_{adj} when processing the same messages during parallel composition. Here, a synchronous output action μ_{in}! is created from an asynchronous input action μ_{in}, or a synchronous input action μ_{out}? is created from an asynchronous output action μ_{out}. The set of clock resets λ is transferred to $S_{TA} \rightarrow S'_{TA}$. Finally, we need to preserve the time intervals in which actions are executed. To that end, the time guard of $S_{TA} \to S'_{TA}$ is the conjunction of the original time guard ρ and the invariant $I(S)$ of S. Thus, $S_{TA} \to S'_{TA}$ is enabled whenever $S \to S'$ is enabled.

Rejecting Insecure Communication. Insecure communication includes two cases: **2a** executing a public action that is not allowed in a location S because no outgoing edge is labeled with it, and **2b** executing a public action that is allowed in S, but violates the timing defined in A_{sec}. For case **2a**, Fig. 4 introduces an edge $S_{TA} \to Err$ for each public action m_{in} or m_{out} that is not allowed in S, i.e., for all actions in $\Sigma_L \setminus \Theta(S)$. The time guard $I(S)$ of these edges ensures that Err is reachable only by actions executed during the activity of S. In contrast to the construction by Heinzemann et al. [30], only public actions make Err reachable. For the opposite case of non-public communication, we add a loop $S_{TA} \to S_{TA}$ for each message that is not in $\Sigma_L \cup \Theta(S)$. Thereby, instead of switching to the Err location, T_A hides all non-public actions that are not allowed.

To handle the timing violations of case **2b**, we create one more edge $S_{TA} \to Err$ labeled with the allowed action μ_{out} or μ_{in} of $S \to S'$. However, this edge is enabled exactly at those times when A_{sec} does not allow the action. To this end, the time guard of the edge is the conjunction of the negated enabling conditions for all edges $S \to S^i$ in A_{sec} that execute the same action as $S \to S'$. The resulting time guard is $\bigwedge_i \neg(\rho_i \wedge I(S))$ where ρ_i is the time guard of $S \to S^i$. Thereby, we ensure that the edge can fire when exceeding the upper bounds of the time intervals in which the action is allowed to execute, or when falling below the lower bounds. In contrast to Heinzemann et al. [30], the edge leads to Err only in case of public messages from Σ_L. For non-public messages, analogously to case **2a**, we construct a loop $S_{TA} \to S_{TA}$. This edge has the same enabling conditions, however, hides the corresponding non-public action instead of switching to Err.

Detecting Absent Communication. Timed noninterference demands that all public actions executable by A_{sec} are executable by the original automaton A in the same time intervals. To check such restrictions, Heinzemann et al. [30] add the constructs labeled with **3** in Fig. 4. We adopt this construction only if μ_{out} or μ_{in} is public (i.e., in Σ_L). In this case, the location R represents a check for required communication. Due to the time guard $\rho \wedge I(S)$, it is reachable during the full time interval in which the edge $S \to S'$ is enabled.

If A preserves the time interval in which A_{sec} can execute the public action, then the edge $R \to N$ is enabled whenever R is entered. The location N represents a neutral state of the analysis that is reachable whenever the required public action is properly executed. N has no outgoing edges because the execution does not have to be further explored from here. Instead, the location S'_{TA} is always reachable when N is reachable and ensures regular execution.

If at some time during its interval, the required public action can not be executed (because A lowers the upper bound or raises its lower bound), then $R \to N$ is not enabled. In this case, the edge $R \to Err$ fires by synchronizing over an auxiliary channel named $fallback$. Synchronization over this channel is always enabled, however, it has the lowest priority compared to all other channels used for communication. Thereby, Err is only reachable when the required public communication is absent.

5   Proof of Concept

In this section, we showcase the utility of our approach in the scope of the example given in Sect. 2.4. To this end, we demonstrate that our technique outperforms the related work by detecting a timing channel that remains undetected using the approach by Barbuti and Tesei [6]. We show that our technique rejects the insecure system, but accepts a mitigated system that is noninterferent.

To verify the information flow security of timed automata, Barbuti and Tesei check that disabling sensitive actions does not affect the reachability of locations. In the scope of our example, the corresponding transformation was shown in Fig. 3a. Clearly, disabling the sensitive submit action does not affect the reachability of locations (compared to Fig. 3b) because all locations are still reachable. Thus, the timing channel described in Sect. 2.4 remains undetected by the approach, and therefore represents a *false negative* because the insecure system is regarded as secure.

In contrast, Fig. 5 illustrates the parallel composition of the adjusted automaton A_{adj} (Fig. 5a) and the test automaton T_a (Fig. 5b) as proposed in this paper. As an artifact for reproduction, we provide a corresponding model that is verifiable by the UPPAAL model checker [23]. Due to lack of space, Fig. 5 merges multiple edges between the same source and target locations into a single edge with alternative synchronization labels. Furthermore, we omit the names of ports over which messages are sent or received. Finally, since edges with a conjunction of actions are not allowed in UPPAAL, we use a *committed* location [10] (labeled with c in Fig. 5) to divide the order and query actions into two consecutive edges. Figure 5 also depicts the additional loops added to both automata for hiding non-public communication, as described for the test automata in Sect. 4.2.

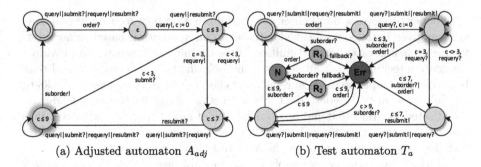

(a) Adjusted automaton A_{adj} (b) Test automaton T_a

Fig. 5. Parallel test system for the motivating example

In the situation depicted in Fig. 5, the system has already processed the message sequence order, query, submit (in the time interval $c < 3$). Since sensitive inputs are disabled in T_a, it can only execute a loop when processing the sensitive submit message. Next, the public suborder message to be sent by A_{adj} corresponds to case ② of our construction in Sect. 4.2. Thus, T_a will regard the message as insecure, and reject it by switching to the Err location. The reason for this violation is that A_{adj} sends the public suborder message too early, i.e., in the time interval $c \in [0, 3]$. Thus, in its current location (cf. Fig. 5b), T_a regards the message as not allowed and switches to Err.

Figure 6 shows the countermeasures taken to mitigate the timing channel. In Fig. 6a, we depict the time guard $c = 9$ added to delay the suborder message. Consequently, the timing of the message does no longer depend on whether or not the product specification was provided over the sensitive internal port. Figure 6b depicts the resulting changes of the test automaton. Since the timing of the suborder message is now fixed, the Err location is no longer reachable. Accordingly, our construction correctly identifies the mitigated system as noninterferent.

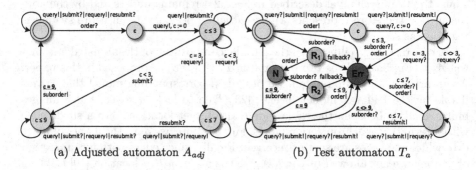

(a) Adjusted automaton A_{adj} (b) Test automaton T_a

Fig. 6. Mitigation of the timing channel in the motivating example

6   Conclusions and Future Work

This paper proposes a novel check for the information flow security of real-time systems given in the form of timed automata. Our approach is based on noninterference as a well-established definition of secure information flow. To provide a verification technique that applies existing tools and takes into account real-time behavior, we adapt the work on refinement checking by Heinzemann et al. [30] to the field of security. We describe the construction of test automata, introducing a dedicated location that indicates violations of noninterference whenever it is reachable during execution. Thereby, we reduce the problem to a reachability test that is supported by model checking techniques used in software engineering practice. In particular, we apply the well-established UPPAAL model checker for timed automata as our underlying verification engine. Our proof of concept demonstrates the advantages of our approach by detecting a timing channel that would remain undetected using the most closely related work.

The proposed idea provides software engineering practitioners with a tool-supported verification technique for the information flow security of timed automata, taking into account specific characteristics of cyber-physical systems like real-time behavior and asynchronous communication. Thereby, we enable engineers to identify information leaks such as timing channels early, and ensure security by design. For cyber-physical systems, this is of vital importance to avoid product recalls or even safety-critical attacks.

Our approach is part of ongoing work on tracing information flow security in cyber-physical systems engineering [22]. In future work, we will provide tool support for our approach in the context of a model-driven software design method for cyber-physical systems. In particular, to check the information flow security of hierarchical component architectures, our work needs to be extended to a compositional verification approach. Thereby, we seek to preserve security when composing overall software systems from single secure components.

Acknowledgments. The authors would like to thank Johannes Geismann and Marie Christin Platenius for helpful comments on drafts of this paper.

References

1. Aceto, L., Burgueño, A., Larsen, K.G.: Model checking via reachability testing for timed automata. In: Steffen, B. (ed.) TACAS 1998. LNCS, vol. 1384, pp. 263–280. Springer, Heidelberg (1998). https://doi.org/10.1007/BFb0054177
2. Agat, J.: Transforming out timing leaks. In: POPL 2000, pp. 40–53. ACM (2000)
3. Akella, R., Tang, H., McMillin, B.M.: Analysis of information flow security in cyber-physical systems. Int. J. Crit. Infrastruct. Prot. **3**(3–4), 157–173 (2010)
4. Alur, R., Courcoubetis, C., Dill, D.L.: Model-checking in dense real-time. Inf. Comput. **104**(1), 2–34 (1993)
5. Alur, R., Dill, D.L.: A theory of timed automata. Theor. Comput. Sci. **126**(2), 183–235 (1994)
6. Barbuti, R., Tesei, L.: A decidable notion of timed non-interference. Fundamenta Informaticae **54**(2–3), 137–150 (2003)
7. Barthe, G., D'Argenio, P.R., Rezk, T.: Secure information flow by self-composition. Math. Struct. Comput. Sci. **21**(6), 1207–1252 (2011)
8. Benattar, G., Cassez, F., Lime, D., Roux, O.H.: Control and synthesis of non-interferent timed systems. Int. J. Control **88**(2), 217–236 (2015)
9. Bengtsson, J., Larsen, K., Larsson, F., Pettersson, P., Yi, W.: UPPAAL—a tool suite for automatic verification of real-time systems. In: Alur, R., Henzinger, T.A., Sontag, E.D. (eds.) HS 1995. LNCS, vol. 1066, pp. 232–243. Springer, Heidelberg (1996). https://doi.org/10.1007/BFb0020949
10. Bengtsson, J., Yi, W.: Timed automata: semantics, algorithms and tools. In: Desel, J., Reisig, W., Rozenberg, G. (eds.) ACPN 2003. LNCS, vol. 3098, pp. 87–124. Springer, Heidelberg (2004). https://doi.org/10.1007/978-3-540-27755-2_3
11. Biswas, A.K., Ghosal, D., Nagaraja, S.: A survey of timing channels and countermeasures. ACM Comput. Surv. **50**(1), 6:1–6:39 (2017)
12. Broman, D., Derler, P., Eidson, J.: Temporal issues in cyber-physical systems. J. Indian Inst. Sci. **93**(3), 389–402 (2013)

13. Cassez, F.: The dark side of timed opacity. In: Park, J.H., Chen, H.-H., Atiquzzaman, M., Lee, C., Kim, T., Yeo, S.-S. (eds.) ISA 2009. LNCS, vol. 5576, pp. 21–30. Springer, Heidelberg (2009). https://doi.org/10.1007/978-3-642-02617-1_3

14. Čerāns, K.: Decidability of bisimulation equivalences for parallel timer processes. In: von Bochmann, G., Probst, D.K. (eds.) CAV 1992. LNCS, vol. 663, pp. 302–315. Springer, Heidelberg (1993). https://doi.org/10.1007/3-540-56496-9_24

15. Chattopadhyay, A., Prakash, A., Shafique, M.: Secure cyber-physical systems: current trends, tools and open research problems. In: DATE 2017, pp. 1104–1109. IEEE (2017)

16. Crnkovic, I., Malavolta, I., Muccini, H., Sharaf, M.: On the use of component-based principles and practices for architecting cyber-physical systems. In: CBSE 2016, pp. 23–32. IEEE (2016)

17. Evans, N., Schneider, S.: Analysing time dependent security properties in CSP using PVS. In: Cuppens, F., Deswarte, Y., Gollmann, D., Waidner, M. (eds.) ESORICS 2000. LNCS, vol. 1895, pp. 222–237. Springer, Heidelberg (2000). https://doi.org/10.1007/10722599_14

18. Finkbeiner, B., Rabe, M.N., Sánchez, C.: Algorithms for model checking HyperLTL and HyperCTL*. In: Kroening, D., Păsăreanu, C.S. (eds.) CAV 2015. LNCS, vol. 9206, pp. 30–48. Springer, Cham (2015). https://doi.org/10.1007/978-3-319-21690-4_3

19. Focardi, R., Gorrieri, R.: A taxonomy of security properties for process algebras. J. Comput. Secur. 3(1), 5–34 (1995)

20. Focardi, R., Gorrieri, R., Martinelli, F.: Real-time information flow analysis. IEEE J. Sel. Areas Commun. 21(1), 20–35 (2003)

21. Focardi, R., Rossi, S., Sabelfeld, A.: Bridging language-based and process calculi security. In: Sassone, V. (ed.) FoSSaCS 2005. LNCS, vol. 3441, pp. 299–315. Springer, Heidelberg (2005). https://doi.org/10.1007/978-3-540-31982-5_19

22. Gerking, C.: Traceability of information flow requirements in cyber-physical systems engineering. In: CEUR Workshop Proceedings, DocSym@MoDELS 2016, vol. 1735 (2016)

23. Gerking, C.: Detection of a timing channel in an UPPAAL model of a cyber-manufacturing system (2018). https://doi.org/10.5281/zenodo.1034024

24. Giacobazzi, R., Mastroeni, I.: Timed abstract non-interference. In: Pettersson, P., Yi, W. (eds.) FORMATS 2005. LNCS, vol. 3829, pp. 289–303. Springer, Heidelberg (2005). https://doi.org/10.1007/11603009_22

25. Giraldo, J., Sarkar, E., Cárdenas, A.A., Maniatakos, M., Kantarcioglu, M.: Security and privacy in cyber-physical systems: a survey of surveys. IEEE Des. Test 34(4), 7–17 (2017)

26. Goguen, J.A., Meseguer, J.: Security policies and security models. In: IEEE S&P, pp. 11–20. IEEE (1982)

27. Goguen, J.A., Meseguer, J.: Unwinding and inference control. In: IEEE S&P, pp. 75–87. IEEE (1984)

28. Gorrieri, R., Lanotte, R., Maggiolo-Schettini, A., Martinelli, F., Tini, S., Tronci, E.: Automated analysis of timed security. Int. J. Inf. Secur. 2(3–4), 168–186 (2004)

29. Guttman, J.D., Nadel, M.E.: What needs securing. In: CSFW, pp. 34–57. MITRE Corporation Press (1988)

30. Heinzemann, C., Brenner, C., Dziwok, S., Schäfer, W.: Automata-based refinement checking for real-time systems. Comput. Sci. - R&D 30(3–4), 255–283 (2015)

31. Kashyap, V., Wiedermann, B., Hardekopf, B.: Timing- and termination-sensitive secure information flow. In: IEEE S&P, pp. 413–428. IEEE (2011)
32. Köpf, B., Basin, D.: Timing-sensitive information flow analysis for synchronous systems. In: Gollmann, D., Meier, J., Sabelfeld, A. (eds.) ESORICS 2006. LNCS, vol. 4189, pp. 243–262. Springer, Heidelberg (2006). https://doi.org/10.1007/11863908_16
33. Lanotte, R., Maggiolo-Schettini, A., Tini, S.: Privacy in real-time systems. Electron. Notes Theor. Comput. Sci. **52**(3), 295–305 (2001)
34. Lanotte, R., Maggiolo-Schettini, A., Troina, A.: Time and probability-based information flow analysis. IEEE Trans. Softw. Eng. **36**(5), 719–734 (2010)
35. Lee, E.A.: CPS foundations. In: DAC 2010, pp. 737–742. ACM (2010)
36. van der Meyden, R., Zhang, C.: Algorithmic verification of noninterference properties. Electron. Notes Theor. Comput. Sci. **168**, 61–75 (2007)
37. van der Meyden, R., Zhang, C.: A comparison of semantic models for noninterference. Theor. Comput. Sci. **411**(47), 4123–4147 (2010)
38. Nguyen, P.H., Ali, S., Yue, T.: Model-based security engineering for cyber-physical systems. Inf. Softw. Technol. **83**, 116–135 (2017)
39. Peisert, S., Margulies, J., Nicol, D.M., Khurana, H., Sawall, C.: Designed-in security for cyber-physical systems. IEEE Secur. Priv. **12**(5), 9–12 (2014)
40. Rafnsson, W., Jia, L., Bauer, L.: Timing-sensitive noninterference through composition. In: Maffei, M., Ryan, M. (eds.) POST 2017. LNCS, vol. 10204, pp. 3–25. Springer, Heidelberg (2017). https://doi.org/10.1007/978-3-662-54455-6_1
41. Roscoe, A.W., Huang, J.: Checking noninterference in timed CSP. Formal Asp. Comput. **25**(1), 3–35 (2013)
42. Sabelfeld, A., Myers, A.C.: Language-based information-flow security. IEEE J. Sel. Areas Commun. **21**(1), 5–19 (2003)
43. Schivo, S., Yildiz, B.M., Ruijters, E., Gerking, C., Kumar, R., Dziwok, S., Rensink, A., Stoelinga, M.: How to efficiently build a front-end tool for UPPAAL: a model-driven approach. In: Larsen, K.G., Sokolsky, O., Wang, J. (eds.) SETTA 2017. LNCS, vol. 10606, pp. 319–336. Springer, Cham (2017). https://doi.org/10.1007/978-3-319-69483-2_19
44. Son, J., Alves-Foss, J.: A formal framework for real-time information flow analysis. Comput. Secur. **28**(6), 421–432 (2009)
45. Vasilikos, P., Nielson, F., Nielson, H.R.: Secure information release in timed automata. In: Bauer, L., Küsters, R. (eds.) POST 2018. LNCS, vol. 10804, pp. 28–52. Springer, Cham (2018). https://doi.org/10.1007/978-3-319-89722-6_2

Off-Limits: Abusing Legacy x86 Memory Segmentation to Spy on Enclaved Execution

Jago Gyselinck, Jo Van Bulck, Frank Piessens, and Raoul Strackx$^{(\boxtimes)}$

imec-DistriNet, KU Leuven,
Celestijnenlaan 200A, 3001 Leuven, Belgium
{jo.vanbulck,frank.piessens,
raoul.strackx}@cs.kuleuven.be,
jago.gyselinck@student.kuleuven.be

Abstract. Enclaved execution environments, such as Intel SGX, enable secure, hardware-enforced isolated execution of critical application components without having to trust the underlying operating system or hypervisor. A recent line of research, however, explores innovative controlled-channel attacks mounted by untrusted system software to partially compromise the confidentiality of enclave programs. Apart from exploiting relatively well-known side-channels like the CPU cache and branch predictor, these attacks have so far focused on tracking side-effects from enclaved address translations via the paging unit.

This paper shows, however, that for 32-bit SGX enclaves the unacclaimed x86 segmentation unit can be abused as a novel controlled-channel to reveal enclaved memory accesses at a page-level granularity, and in restricted circumstances even at a very precise byte-level granularity. While the x86 paging unit has been extensively studied from both an attack as well as a defense perspective, we are the first to show that address translation side-channels are not limited to paging. Our findings furthermore confirm that largely abandoned legacy x86 processor features, included for backwards compatibility, suggest new and unexpected side-channels.

Keywords: Intel SGX · Controlled-channel · x86 · Paging
Segmentation

1 Introduction

Most popular operating systems and virtual machine managers have now been around for multiple decades. During this period, a steady stream of critical

---

The stamp on the top of this paper refers to an approval process conducted by the ESSoS Artifact Evaluation Committee.

vulnerabilities has been found in their expansive code bases. These vulnerabilities continue to be problematic for any application that wishes to do secure computations on such a platform. In order to shield applications from potentially malicious or compromised system software, a significant research effort has recently been put into creating Protected Module Architectures (PMAs) [7,16,17,22]. These architectures offer isolated execution for security sensitive application components, while leaving the underlying system software explicitly untrusted. With the introduction of its Software Guard Extensions (SGX) [1,6,17], Intel brought their implementation of a PMA to the mass consumer market. Conceived as an extension to the x86 instruction set architecture, SGX provides strong trusted computing guarantees with a minimal Trusted Computing Base (TCB), which is limited to the protected module or *enclave*, and the processor package.

Recent research [15,18,21,24–27] has shown, however, that the combination of SGX's strong adversary model and reduced TCB allows a privileged attacker to create high resolution, low-noise *controlled-channels* that leak information about the enclave's internal state. More specifically, enclave programs still rely on the untrusted operating system to manage shared platform resources such as CPU time or memory. Within SGX's adversary model, an attacker may attempt to leverage control over these resources to infer enclave secrets. Notably, Xu et al. [27] first showed how to recover rich information such as full images and text from a single enclaved execution by carefully restricting enclave page access rights and observing the resulting page fault sequences. Since their seminal work, more conventional side-channels such as the processor cache [2,10,18] and branch prediction unit [15] have also been improved in the context of SGX.

Considering that innovative page fault attacks [21,27] only recently became relevant in a kernel-level PMA adversary model, they have received considerable attention from the research community. A good level of understanding of page table attack surface has since been built up by *(i)* exploring stealthy attack variants [25,26] that abuse other side-effects of the page table walk, *(ii)* developing software-based defense mechanisms [4,5,20,23] for off-the-shelf SGX processors, and *(iii)* designing fortified PMAs [7,8] that rule out these attacks at the hardware level. This paper shows, however, that enclaved memory accesses in 32-bit mode not only leak through page tables, but also through the largely overlooked x86 memory segmentation unit. A feature that is for the most part disabled on 64-bit systems, but regains relevance when considering 32-bit enclaves. We advance the understanding of address translation controlled-channels by showing that under certain assumptions, attackers can leverage control over segment limits to infer byte-granular memory access patterns from an enclaved execution. Furthermore, our findings illustrate that the backwards compatibility requirement of modern x86 processors suggests new and unexpected side-channels stemming from largely abandoned legacy features. In summary, the contributions of this paper are:

- We show how for 32-bit enclaves the x86 segmentation unit can be abused as a novel, noise-free side-channel to reveal precise byte-granular control flow and instruction sizes in the first megabyte of a victim enclave.

- We explain how for the remainder of the enclave address space, segmentation attacks can infer memory accesses at a conventional page-level granularity.
- We implement our attacks and practically demonstrate their enhanced precision by defeating a recently proposed branch obfuscation defense.
- We reveal an undocumented Intel microcode update that silently blocks our attacks without updating the processor's security version number. Only the very recent Spectre CPU updates can adequately prevent our attacks.

2   Background

We first present Intel SGX and our attacker model, before introducing the necessary background on x86 memory organization.

2.1   Intel SGX and Adversary Model

Recent Intel processors include an architectural extension called the Software Guard Extensions (SGX) [1,11,17] which bring strong, processor-enforced confidentiality and integrity guarantees for protected software modules called *enclaves*. SGX enclaves live inside a conventional OS process, and span a contiguous virtual address range (ELRANGE) for their protected code and data. The processor's memory access control logic takes care to block any access to ELRANGE from outside the corresponding enclave, regardless of the current CPU privilege level. Furthermore, to prevent active memory mapping attacks [6] performed by a kernel-level attacker in control of page table mappings, the processor verifies that every physical enclave address is accessed via the expected virtual address.

SGX includes several new x86 instructions to switch the processor in and out of enclave mode. EENTER allows to transfer control to a specific point in the enclave, while its counterpart EEXIT returns control flow back to untrusted memory. In case of an interrupt or fault during enclaved execution, an Asynchronous Enclave eXit (AEX) occurs. Much like leaving an enclave, AEX saves the enclave's state to later be resumed, while again clearing any processor state that may leak information. After the reason for the interrupt has been serviced, the enclave can be resumed using the ERESUME instruction.

SGX considers even the kernel as potentially malicious. Our attacks assume a less powerful attacker; we show that user-level capabilities suffice to control the segmentation unit. However, as will be indicated in our attack descriptions, we make use of a secondary framework to execute our attacks. While these are often interchangeable, some require a more privileged attacker. In case such a secondary framework is chosen, the attacker model should be upgraded accordingly. In general, we also assume the attacker has access to the enclave's object code, unless explicitly stated otherwise.

At the system level, we focus exclusively on 32-bit enclaves, for segmentation is practically disabled in 64-bit mode. Furthermore, as discussed in more detail in Sect. 5, we assume the processor runs one of the vulnerable microcode versions listed in Appendix A.

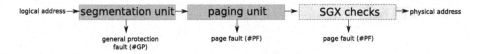

Fig. 1. On x86 logical addresses pass through the segmentation and paging units respectively. The resulting physical address is additionally sanitized by SGX.

2.2 x86 Memory Management

To enable SGX enclaves to be easily integrated in legacy applications, they live in the same address space. Unfortunately this implies that the architectural complexities of x86 memory organization play a crucial role in assessing SGX's isolation properties [6]. Memory management in the IA-32 architecture [11] proceeds via two distinct hardware components, visualized in Fig. 1. Application software uses *logical* addresses, which are first passed through a dedicated segmentation unit to yield *linear* addresses as an input to the paging unit. SGX finally enforces some (limited) additional checks on the resulting *physical* addresses.

The Segmentation Unit. Segmentation serves as a way to divide the logical address space into segments. The x86 hardware provides 6 *segment registers* (%CS, %DS, %SS, %ES, %FS and %GS) to directly reference segments. Each machine instruction either explicitly references a segment register, or one is implied. Pushing or popping data from the stack, for example, always references the stack segment (%SS). Similarly, the instruction pointer (%eip) is always relative to the code segment (%CS). Move instructions to memory always imply the data segment (%DS). Segments %FS and %GS are typically used for thread-local storage.

Figure 2 displays how the segmentation unit operates during the execution of an instruction. For each segment referenced, its *segment descriptor* is located in the Local Descriptor Table (LDT) or Global Descriptor Table (GDT). Each descriptor records the base (linear) address of the segment, its limit and the associated access rights (i.e., read, write, execute). When the instruction does not violate the access rights to the segment, and the logical address remains within the segment limits, the linear address is calculated by adding the segment base to the logical address. Otherwise a General Protection fault (#GP) is issued.

In 32-bit mode segment descriptors measure only 64 bits in size. This is too limited to store 32-bit base and limit addresses, plus other attributes (e.g., access rights). To resolve this issue, only a 20-bit limit field is used in combination with a special *granularity* bit. When this bit is clear, limits can be specified up to $2^{20} - 1$ (1 MiB) at byte granularity. Otherwise the limit field is interpreted at 4 KiB granularity, allowing the logical address space to reach $(2^{20} - 1) * 4096$. As the 12 least significant bits of this limit are not checked, the full 2^{32} address space can be accessed [11, Sect. 5.3].

Over time, segmentation has evolved to become more and more obsolete. In 64-bit mode, the processor ignores the segment descriptor registers for %DS, %SS and %ES, limit checks are no longer performed and the base of %CS is always treated as zero. [11, Sect. 3.4]

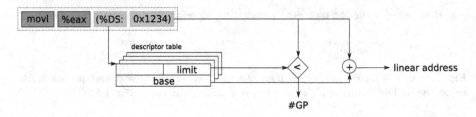

Fig. 2. The segmentation unit checks that each referenced segment adheres to the segment's limitations described in the descriptor table

The Paging Unit. After the segmentation unit translated a logical address to a linear one, the paging unit translates it in turn to a physical address. It does so by dividing the linear address space in fixed memory regions called pages. The base address of each referenced page is located in an in-memory page table structure maintained by the operating system. After the page table walk, the processor obtains the physical page base address, plus the associated access rights and other attributes (e.g., whether the page is present or has been accessed before).

3   Segmentation-Based Attacks

Intel SGX enclaves execute in the same logical address space as their host process. Just like logical addresses used in the untrusted (legacy) part of a process pass through the segmentation and paging unit, so do the addresses referenced during SGX enclave execution. These address translation units are under complete control of the potentially malicious kernel. To prevent an attacker from mistranslating enclave addresses, Intel SGX applies additional checks as a final step (see Fig. 1). During enclave creation, the processor records for every enclave page the logical address they should be loaded at and to which physical address they should be translated to. The kernel is still in control over all memory allocation decisions. She can for example decide to evict enclave pages from main memory, but the hardware will check whether the memory translation units have been set up correctly.

Unfortunately, SGX's untrusted page table design also opens up powerful controlled-channel attacks. Early page fault-driven attacks [21,27] and more recently improved fault-less page table-based attacks [25,26] show that paging mechanisms can be abused by an attacker to leak enclave memory accesses at page-level granularity. When these memory accesses are secret-dependent, they may reveal sensitive information. To the best of our knowledge, academic research has only looked into leveraging the paging unit. For an SGX-capable processor in 32-bit mode however, the segmentation unit also interposes on every enclaved address translation.

3.1   Interaction Between Segmentation and SGX

The Intel Programming Reference Manual [12] states that "enclaves abide by all the segmentation policies set up by the OS", but several sanity checks on the segmentation policy have been put in place. For example, it is enforced that the %CS, %DS, %SS and %ES registers point to segment descriptors which have their base address set to zero, as any other value could maliciously change the interpretation of enclaved code. Trusted in-enclave segment selectors and descriptors for the %FS and %GS segments are saved and replaced on enclave entry to facilitate access to the enclave's thread local storage. This means that the %FS and %GS segments are immune to the attacks described in this paper, for any modifications made by an attacker will not propagate to enclaved execution.

We make the crucial observation that, while the Intel SGX hardware forces segment descriptor base addresses to be 0x0, their limit is still under the control of an attacker. Reducing the limit of a segment, will cause a general protection fault whenever an attempt is made to cross it. In Sect. 2.2 we have discussed that segment limits can be specified at byte-granularity up to the 1 MiB boundary. Limits past this bound can only be specified at 4 KiB granularity.

3.2   Attack #1: Page Granular Attacks

We will first explore the possibilities when the granularity flag is set. As said before, this will allow to leak information about memory accesses at page granularity. When compared to the earlier explored page fault-driven attacks, there is one fundamental difference. Restricting page access rights makes small chunks of memory inaccessible for the processor, while leaving others completely unaffected. Segmentation presents a rougher, binary condition; either a memory location is within the segment or it is not. In other words, moving the segment limit not only influences a single page, but all pages that are now above the segment limit.

It is this difference that presents an interesting challenge. We present a running example code snippet in Fig. 3 with some sample enclave code that represents a simple voting mechanism. We assume the vote being cast is secret and that the attacker wishes to derive its value. For simplicity we assume all functions of interest are aligned on their own pages. To illustrate the problem, imagine the vote function being executed, with the segment limit taken as indicated on Fig. 3. Now assume that the attacker observes a general protection fault. Clearly, this may occur when the vote function was called for candidate B, as the handler for that candidate is outside of the segment. However, a second possibility also exists where the vote is for candidate A. Here, control will be passed back to the vote function, which in turn calls the total vote handler, causing a general protection fault as well. The two general protection faults will be identical to an attacker, who is now unable to derive any information. To solve this, we combine the segmentation unit with a secondary framework. In most of our examples, we use the page-fault side-channel as an extra layer of information for simplicity of illustration. This side-channel then functions as an oracle to indicate to the

```
1   void vote(enum candidate c) {
2       if (c == candidate_a)
3           handle_candidate_a();
4       else
5           handle_candidate_b();
6       handle_total_votes();
7       return;
8   }
9
10  void handle_candidate_a() {
11      candidate_a_votes++;
12  }
13
14  void handle_candidate_b() {
15      candidate_b_votes++;
16  }
17
18  void handle_total_votes() {
19      total_votes++;
20  }
```

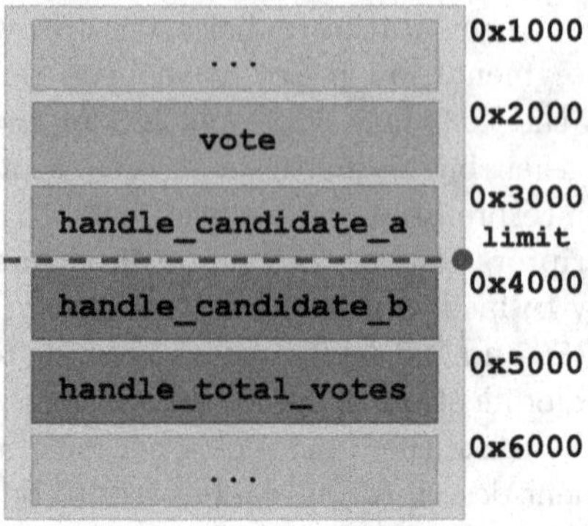

Fig. 3. Example enclave with secret dependent control transfer.

attacker whether the memory access has passed the segmentation stage. The exact same can also be achieved by monitoring the page accessed bit [25,26]. Alternatively, we can make sure the enclave takes just one step, for which a single stepping interrupt framework such as SGX-Step [24] can be used.

Since this first attack has the same granularity as the original page fault driven attacks, it would not be useful in this context to use that same side-channel as the secondary framework. At the same time, replicating previous page table-based attacks results [21,25–27] without using the paging unit demonstrates that state-of-the-art defenses that move the page tables into enclave memory [7,8] may not suffice for 32-bit enclaves. Because of this, we illustrate how we can replicate page fault-driven attacks using solely the segmentation unit and SGX-Step, without the need to alter page table entries.

Reconsider the running example of Fig. 3, where we wish to extract which candidate was voted for. Initially, we set the limit of %CS at 0x3000, making pages of both candidate handlers inaccessible. The attacker is then guaranteed to observe a general protection fault when the enclave is single stepped until one of the handlers is called. At this point, the attacker can move the segment limit to also include the handler for candidate A (limit at 0x4000). When the enclave is resumed, the single-stepping framework makes sure at most one instruction is executed, after which two situations can be distinguished:

1. No fault is observed, which indicates that the vote was for candidate A. Control is successfully passed to the handler for that candidate, which is located within the segment.
2. A second general protection fault is observed. This indicates that the vote was for candidate B, as only a call to this function crosses the segment boundary.

Table 1. Segmentation plus paging configurations and whether they generate a General Protection fault (#GP) or Page Fault (#PF).

eip $\leq$ limit	page access rights	(eip + inst size) $\leq$ limit	Fault type
✗	-	-	#GP$_1$
✓	✓	✗	#GP$_2$
✓	✗	-	#PF

3.3   Precise Byte Granular Attacks

In this section, we present the most fine-grained attacks that are possible using the segmentation unit. Keep in mind that these are also the attacks with the most limitations. Again, they are applicable to 32-bit enclaves only, where the region of interest to the attacker is located within the first megabyte of the victim enclave's memory layout.

The segmentation and paging unit are closely integrated. While conceptually they can be regarded as executing one after the other at the architectural level (see Fig. 1), we found this to be inaccurate at the microarchitectural level. We will show that by carefully setting segment limits and page rights, detailed information about the control flow and even instruction sizes leak to an attacker.

Combining the Segmentation and Paging Units. Only when an instruction is completely contained within the limits of the code segment, it may execute. When the instruction falls outside the code segment's limit, a #GP is generated. An interesting edge case occurs, however, when a multi-byte instruction starts within the code segment, but passes its boundaries. In that case, the fault thrown depends on the paging unit: only when the page the instruction is located on has execute permissions, a #GP is thrown. Otherwise, the paging unit generates a Page Fault (#PF). This behavior is summarized in Table 1.

We conclude that the segmentation and paging units verify access rights and limits in parallel at the microarchitectural level. We suspect that the exact outcome may differ between different processor generations and models, but always found stable outcomes on a single machine.

Attack #2: Inferring Instruction Sizes. Previous enclaved execution side-channel attacks [2,15,18,25,27] rely on static analysis of the victim enclave's source code. In some cases however, the object code of the enclave may not be available to the attacker or it may be randomized on enclave load [19]. If so, it may be of interest to the attacker to learn as much as possible about the instructions that are being executed [14]. For example, when code is randomized, this information may reveal the location of crucial functions by comparing the leaked outline to the non-randomized object code. To this end, we contribute a novel approach to infer enclaved instruction sizes by leveraging the segmentation and paging units and applying the techniques mentioned before.

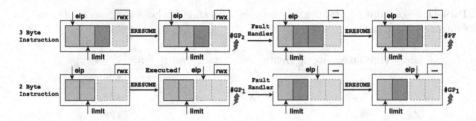

Fig. 4. Fault sequence attack to infer instruction size (three vs. two bytes).

To infer instruction sizes, we retake the idea of having two layers of information: the segmentation and the paging unit. An intuitive approach would be to take the segment limit at the start of an instruction, while revoking the access rights to the underlying page. Surely, this leads to a first general protection fault, as the instruction falls outside of the segment. In consecutive steps, we may gradually increase the segment limit with a single byte, until we observe a page fault. This would imply that the whole instruction is now within the segment, thus also revealing the instruction size. However, as explained above, the x86 segmentation and paging units work in parallel at the hardware level. We experimentally confirmed that including the first byte of an instruction into the segment is enough to activate the paging unit. As a result, as long as the underlying page access rights are revoked, a page fault will be reported regardless of instruction size.

Our practical attack therefore combines information leakage from both the paging and segmentation units. Figure 4 illustrates how an attacker can distinguish an exemplary three-byte instruction from a two-byte one. Initially, after interrupting the enclave before the instruction of interest, we set the code segment limit to include two bytes of the instruction about to be executed, and assign read/write/execute permissions to the underlying page. Next, the enclave is continued through the ERESUME instruction, and we observe a general protection fault $\#GP_1$ or $\#GP_2$, depending on whether the code segment limit violation was caused by either the current or the next instruction.[1] At this point, however, the attacker has no way of distinguishing $\#GP_1$ and $\#GP_2$, as both show up as identical general protection faults raised by the segmentation unit.

To overcome this challenge, we introduce the notion of *fault sequence attacks* as a novel generalization of the page fault sequences originally presented by Xu et al. [27]. That is, before resuming the victim enclave a second time, we configure the code segment limit to include the first byte of the instruction of interest and revoke access rights to the underlying page. According to Table 1, we now only observe a #GP when the secret in-enclave instruction pointer falls outside of the code segment. In case the enclaved instruction was larger than two bytes, on the other hand, the instruction pointer was not incremented and a #PF will be

---

[1] Note that we assume here that the next instruction is located immediately after the current one in memory. We explain in the next section how segmentation-based attacks can infer secret target addresses in case of jump instructions.

```
void foo(unsigned int secret) {        1  push   %ebp
    if (secret)                        2  mov    %esp,%ebp
        asm __volatile__("nop");       3  cmp    $0x0,0x8(%ebp)
    else                               4  je     7 <foo+0xc>
        asm __volatile__("nop");       5  nop
}                                      6  jmp    8 <foo+0xd>
                                       7  nop
                                       8  pop    %ebp
                                       9  ret
```

Fig. 5. Using byte-granular segment limits, we can infer very precise control flow.

observed since the first byte of the instruction is included in the code segment. As such, our approach observes the *combined sequence* of general protection and page faults to infer the secret in-enclave instruction pointer.

Attack #3: Inferring Branch Target Addresses. When we are able to set segmentation limits with a byte-level granularity, we can infer much more fine-grained control flow than page-unit-based attacks [21,25–27]. Consider the C code of Fig. 5 and its translation to assembly. Even though the condition of secret results in the execution of only a few different instructions, we are able to infer which branch is taken and thus the boolean value of secret.

An attacker could first interrupt enclave execution by retracting the access rights of the page on which the "foo" function is located. Next, the page access rights can be restored, while lowering the segment limit to exclude any instruction past line 4 in the assembly listing. Placing the segment limit at this address excludes both control flow branches while just including the je (i.e., "jump equal") instruction.

Regardless of the value of secret, a general protection fault will occur when the enclave is resumed. When secret evaluates to false, the cmp (i.e., "compare") instruction on line 3 will have set the equal flag. Executing the je instruction on line 4 will then result in a #GP fault as the jump destination crosses the segment boundary. When the enclave is resumed after the fault is handled, another attempt will be made to execute the je instruction.

Alternatively, the secret evaluates to true. In that case the jump will not be taken. A general protection fault is issued as line 5's nop (i.e., "no-operation") instruction is (completely) located past the code segment's bounds.

To distinguish the two cases, we again rely on the paging unit and leverage the differences in microarchitectural behavior when an instruction is located in- or outside of the code segment on a non-executable page. Specifically, we revoke access rights to the underlying page, while leaving the segment limit untouched. When the enclave is resumed, two cases can occur:

– **General protection fault is issued:** This implies that the instruction must be located past the limits of the code segment. Hence, the enclave attempted to execute the `nop` instruction on line 5. This could only occur when `secret` was `true` and the `cmp` instruction cleared the equal flag.

– **Page fault is issued:** This is similar to non-branching instructions that are located on a non-executable page within the code segment. Conditional jump instructions will also lead to a #PF when they are located within the code segment, even when their target points outside the code segment. Hence, we can derive that the `je` instruction attempts to continue execution at its specified target. This implies that the `cmp` instruction cleared the equal flag, and thus `secret` was `false`.

The above mechanism only works when targeting forward jump instructions. With backward jumps, execution will branch within the segment and another approach is required. We discuss this in more detail in the following section.

4 A Practical End-to-End Attack Scenario

In this section, we present a practical attack scenario that exploits the increased attack surface stemming from the x86 segmentation unit. Specifically, we show how the ability to infer precise byte-granular control flow information (attack variant #3) defeats state-of-the-art branch prediction hardening techniques.

Recent research on *branch shadowing* attacks [15] demonstrated that fine-grained enclave-private control flow leaks through the CPU-internal branch target buffer. This work also included a compile-time defense scheme called Zigzagger. The key idea, illustrated in Fig. 6, is to obfuscate secret-dependent target addresses via an oblivious `cmove` (i.e., "conditional move") instruction,[2] followed by a tight trampoline sequence of unconditional jumps that ends with a single indirect branch instruction. Zigzagger's security argument relies on the observation that *(i)* the branch shadowing attack in itself cannot directly infer the target address of the indirect branch at `zz4`, plus *(ii)* recognizing the unconditional jumps `zz1` to `zz3` becomes considerably more challenging when rapidly jumping back and forth between the instrumented code and the trampoline. Previous research on precise interrupt-driven attacks [24] has shown that condition *(ii)* is insufficient for an SGX attacker that can reliably single-step enclaved execution. To date, however, no practical attack demonstration against Zigzagger-instrumented code has been presented. We show that, when the hardened code lives in the first megabyte of a 32-bit victim enclave, condition *(i)* additionally does not hold, for general protection faults deterministically reveal the secret-dependent indirect branch target address.

We attack the Zigzagger defense by combining our segmentation attacks with SGX-Step [24]. We first revoke access rights for the page on which the Zigzagger code is located. This provides us with a starting point where we can set up our attack. Initially, we want the instrumented code to execute up to the secret

---

[2] The `cmove` instruction packs a condition and move into a single instruction. The move is only performed when the equal flag in the processor's status register is set.

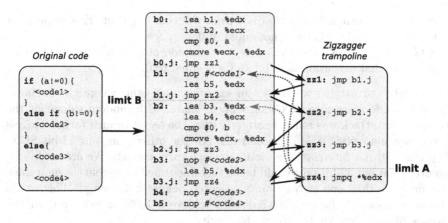

Fig. 6. Example code snippet [15] protected by Zigzagger. The secret branch address in edx is obfuscated with cmov and a tight jmp trampoline sequence.

dependent jump in zz4. As the Zigzagger trampoline is located above the instrumented code in memory, we can achieve this by lowering the code segment limit to exclude zz4 (limit A in Fig. 6). Once page access rights have been restored, the enclave is resumed, after which a general protection fault is observed when execution reaches zz4. At this point a secret dependent jump is about to be made. Note that with segmentation alone, determining which branch will be taken is not possible, as lowering the segment limit to exclude any of the two secret dependent branches also excludes the jump instruction. This is where we require a secondary framework. By using SGX-Step's precise interrupt capabilities we can make sure that if we reset the segment limit and resume the enclave, at most one instruction is executed. The interrupt can also arrive early, however, after which a zero-step is taken meaning no enclaved instructions are executed. Because of this, the attacker should verify on the next interrupt whether the jump in zz4 has executed. To do this, we revoke access rights to the page on which the Zigzagger code is located, as well as lowering the segment limit to exclude zz4 (limit A in Fig. 6). Next, two types of faults can occur:

- **#PF:** The current instruction is within the segment, as we can pass the segmentation stage. A page fault occurs because the access rights for the underlying page have been revoked.
- **#GP:** zz4 is still being executed, the indirect branch instruction is outside of the code segment, causing a general protection fault. This indicates that the interrupt arrived too early, causing a zero-step. In this case, we can simply retry the single-stepping process above.

Once it has been established that the jump has been executed, we can execute a final test to see which one of the branches has been jumped to. We keep page access rights revoked, but lower the segment limit to now also exclude all Zigzagger code from b2 on (limit B in Fig. 6). When the enclave is resumed, again two types of faults may occur, following the same pattern as above:

- **#PF:** The current instruction is within the code segment. Execution is at b1, also indicating that a is not equal to 0.
- **#GP:** The current instruction is now outside of the code segment. This indicates that execution is at b2 and a is equal to 0.

To evaluate our attack, we create an experimental setup where the enclaved Zigzagger code is executed 1000 subsequent times, with random values for the secret a. Our attack was able to correctly infer the secret branch target address in the vast majority (98%) of those runs. For the other runs, our 32-bit SGX-Step port did not interrupt the victim enclave early enough. We are confident, however, that our 32-bit port could be further fine-tuned to uphold the guarantee that no more than one instruction is executed before an interrupt. This would eliminate misses of the attack window to achieve a 100% success rate, at the expense of more interrupts arriving too early.

5   Discussion and Mitigations

Our work shows that for 32-bit enclaves, the attack surface from address translation is *not* limited to paging, but also encompasses the often overlooked x86 segmentation unit. This finding may have profound consequences for state-of-the-art defenses [7,8] that move page table memory out of reach of an attacker. Indeed, we showed that page-granular access patterns can be revealed without altering page table entries (attack variant #1). Moreover, we demonstrated that memory accesses in the first megabyte of a 32-bit enclave are additionally vulnerable to very precise byte-granular segmentation-based attacks. We showed how this ability (variant #3) can be abused to directly circumvent innovative control flow obfuscation hardening techniques [15], and can be leveraged to infer instruction sizes (variant #2). The latter may in turn break fine-grained, in-enclave address space layout randomization techniques [19].

Our attacks are restricted to 32-bit enclaves only, as x86 processors practically disable segmentation in 64-bit mode. At this point in time, it is hard to estimate how wide-spread 32-bit enclaves are, or eventually will be. SGX is still a developing technology and only time will tell whether people wish to enclave their legacy 32-bit software. While this assuredly limits the applicability of segmentation-based attacks, it also confirms an important hypothesis. Namely, that supporting 32-bit enclave software in the interest of backwards compatibility may introduce unexpected security vulnerabilities – as has been suggested before [6]. Exploring such legacy aspects could furthermore bring valuable insights for the design and verification of novel hardware-software PMA co-designs [7,9]. As such, we encourage further research to explore the additional attack surface stemming from enclave interaction with legacy x86 features.

While developing our attack framework, we found that recent Intel microcode updates silently address segmentation-based attacks against 32-bit enclaves. Remarkedly, we could not find any official Intel reference that documents this behavior, and can only hypothesize on the extra security checks. Specifically, we found that the patched EENTER/ERESUME instructions now immediately fault whenever any of the segment limits fall within `ELRANGE`. While this effectively prevents all attack variants #1 to #3, we confirmed that the current solution still leaves (limited) segmentation-based attack surface. That is, an adversary can still detect the *use* of a particular segment by setting the segment limit to exclude the enclave base address, and observing a general protection fault whenever the segment is accessed during the enclaved execution. Since `%CS/DS` are always referenced on enclave entry, and `%FS/GS` are loaded from a trusted in-enclave data structure, only the use of `%SS/ES` can be established in this manner.

We had to fall back to manual testing to identify vulnerable microcode versions. Our results are summarized in Appendix A. As a crucial observation, however, we found that the relevant microcode updates do *not* increase the CPU Security Version Number (CPUSVN), which reflects the processor's TCB measurement for local and remote enclave attestations [1]. Importantly, since SGX's attacker model assumes a potentially malicious kernel, microcode revisions that do not increase CPUSVN can be silently rolled back without alerting the victim enclave or remote stakeholder. Only the very recent Spectre [3,13] microcode patches increase CPUSVN and adequately prevent our attacks. Our findings therefore provide additional evidence that (32-bit) enclave attestations with a pre-Spectre CPUSVN should be considered untrustworthy.

6 Conclusion

Recent research on Intel SGX side-channel attacks has focused on the paging unit, caches and branch target buffer. In this paper we have looked into a previously unexplored hardware component: the segmentation unit. We found that for 32-bit enclaves, segmentation-based attacks may reveal security sensitive information. By combining microarchitectural behavior originating from the interplay between the IA-32 segmentation and paging unit, our generalized notion of fault sequence attacks can infer very detailed information. When a 32-bit enclave uses the first 1 MiB of its address space, fine-grained control flow plus instruction sizes can be leaked to an attacker. We furthermore showed how segmentation-based attacks additionally reveal memory accesses past the 1 MiB boundary at a conventional page-level granularity.

We found that Intel has silently patched segmentation-based enclave attack surface, but without updating the CPUSVN number. This implies that kernel-level attackers are able to rollback the microcode revisions unnoticed, until SGX remote attestation schemes reject attestation reports of processors with old microcode revisions. Only with the very recent microcode patches that address the Spectre attacks, will the CPUSVN number be increased and exploitation of the segmentation unit be adequately prevented.

Responsible Disclosure and Availability. We responsibly disclosed our results to Intel and a microcode patch has been distributed. To ensure the reproducibility of our results, and to encourage future research that explores 32-bit enclave vulnerabilities, we have made the full source code of our segmentation attack framework, 32-bit SGX-Step port, and SGX SDK runtime modifications publicly available.[3]

Acknowledgements. This work was partially supported by the Research Fund KU Leuven. Jo Van Bulck and Raoul Strackx are supported by a grant of the Research Foundation – Flanders (FWO).

A   Vulnerable Microcode Versions

Only very recently, Intel provided microcode revisions to foil our segmentation-based attacks. We tested the following microcode revisions for our Skylake machine:

Version	Release date	CPUSVN	Vulnerable
0x1E	unknown	020202ffffff00000000000000000000	Yes
0x2E	unknown	020202ffffff00000000000000000000	Yes
0x9E	unknown	020202ffffff00000000000000000000	Yes
0x4A	unknown	020202ffffff00000000000000000000	Yes
0x8A	unknown	020202ffffff00000000000000000000	Yes
0xBA	April 9th, 2017	020202ffffff00000000000000000000	No
0xC2	November 16th, 2017	020702ffffff00000000000000000000	No

References

1. Anati, I., Gueron, S., Johnson, S., Scarlata, V.: Innovative technology for CPU based attestation and sealing. In: Proceedings of the 2nd International Workshop on Hardware and Architectural Support for Security and Privacy, vol. 13. ACM, New York (2013)
2. Brasser, F., Müller, U., Dmitrienko, A., Kostiainen, K., Capkun, S., Sadeghi, A.-R.: Software grand exposure: SGX cache attacks are practical. In: 11th USENIX Workshop on Offensive Technologies (WOOT 2017). USENIX Association, Vancouver (2017)
3. Chen, G., Chen, S., Xiao, Y., Zhang, Y., Lin, Z., Lai, T.H.: SgxPectre attacks: leaking enclave secrets via speculative execution. arXiv preprint arXiv:1802.09085 (2018)
4. Chen, G., Wang, W., Chen, T., Chen, S., Zhang, Y., Wang, X., Lai, T.-H., Lin, D.: Racing in hyperspace: closing hyper-threading side channels on SGX with contrived data races. In: 2018 IEEE Symposium on Security and Privacy (SP). IEEE (2018)
5. Chen, S., Zhang, X., Reiter, M.K., Zhang, Y.: Detecting privileged side-channel attacks in shielded execution with déjà vu. In: Proceedings of the 2017 Asia Conference on Computer and Communications Security, Asia CCS 2017, pp. 7–18. ACM (2017)

---

[3] https://distrinet.cs.kuleuven.be/software/off-limits/.

6. Costan, V., Devadas, S.: Intel SGX explained. IACR Cryptology ePrint Archive, 2016:86 (2016)
7. Costan, V., Lebedev, I., Devadas, S.: Sanctum: minimal hardware extensions for strong software isolation. In: 25th USENIX Security Symposium (USENIX Security 2016), pp. 857–874. USENIX Association, Austin (2016)
8. Evtyushkin, D., Elwell, J., Ozsoy, M., Ponomarev, D., Ghazaleh, N.A., Riley, R.: Iso-X: a flexible architecture for hardware-managed isolated execution. In: 2014 47th Annual IEEE/ACM International Symposium on Microarchitecture, pp. 190–202, December 2014
9. Ferraiuolo, A., Baumann, A., Hawblitzel, C., Parno, B.: Komodo: using verification to disentangle secure-enclave hardware from software. In: Proceedings of the 26th Symposium on Operating Systems Principles. ACM (2017)
10. Götzfried, J., Eckert, M., Schinzel, S., Müller, T.: Cache attacks on Intel SGX. In: Proceedings of the 10th European Workshop on Systems Security (EuroSec 2017) (2017)
11. Intel Corporation: Intel® 64 and IA-32 Architectures Software Developer's Manual (2017)
12. Intel Corporation: Intel® Software Guard Extensions Programming Reference (2017)
13. Kocher, P., Genkin, D., Gruss, D., Haas, W., Hamburg, M., Lipp, M., Mangard, S., Prescher, T., Schwarz, M., Yarom, Y.: Spectre attacks: exploiting speculative execution. ArXiv e-prints, January 2018
14. Lee, J., Jang, J., Jang, Y., Kwak, N., Choi, Y., Choi, C., Kim, T., Peinado, M., Kang, B.B.: Hacking in darkness: return-oriented programming against secure enclaves. In: 26th USENIX Security Symposium (USENIX Security 2017), pp. 523–539. USENIX Association (2017)
15. Lee, S., Shih, M.-W., Gera, P., Kim, T., Kim, H., Peinado, M.: Inferring fine-grained control flow inside SGX enclaves with branch shadowing. In: 26th USENIX Security Symposium (USENIX Security 2017), pp. 557–574. USENIX Association, Vancouver (2017)
16. Maene, P., Gotzfried, J., De Clercq, R., Muller, T., Freiling, F., Verbauwhede, I.: Hardware-based trusted computing architectures for isolation and attestation. IEEE Trans. Comput. (2017)
17. McKeen, F., Alexandrovich, I., Berenzon, A., Rozas, C.V., Shafi, H., Shanbhogue, V., Savagaonkar, U.R.: Innovative instructions and software model for isolated execution. In: Proceedings of the 2nd International Workshop on Hardware and Architectural Support for Security and Privacy, HASP 2013, p. 10:1. ACM, New York (2013). https://doi.org/10.1145/2487726.2488368
18. Schwarz, M., Weiser, S., Gruss, D., Maurice, C., Mangard, S.: Malware guard extension: using SGX to conceal cache attacks. In: Polychronakis, M., Meier, M. (eds.) DIMVA 2017. LNCS, vol. 10327, pp. 3–24. Springer, Cham (2017). https://doi.org/10.1007/978-3-319-60876-1_1
19. Seo, J., Lee, B., Kim, S., Shih, M.-W., Shin, I., Han, D., Kim, T.: SGX-shield: enabling address space layout randomization for SGX programs. In: Proceedings of the 2017 Annual Network and Distributed System Security Symposium (NDSS), San Diego, CA (2017)
20. Shih, M.-W., Lee, S., Kim, T., Peinado, M.: T-SGX: eradicating controlled-channel attacks against enclave programs. In: 24th Annual Network and Distributed System Security Symposium (NDSS) (2017)

21. Shinde, S., Chua, Z.L., Narayanan, V., Saxena, P.: Preventing page faults from telling your secrets. In: Proceedings of the 11th ACM on Asia Conference on Computer and Communications Security (ASIA CCS), pp. 317–328. ACM (2016)

22. Strackx, R., Noorman, J., Verbauwhede, I., Preneel, B., Piessens, F.: Protected software module architectures. In: Reimer, H., Pohlmann, N., Schneider, W. (eds.) ISSE 2013 Securing Electronic Business Processes, pp. 241–251. Springer, Wiesbaden (2013). https://doi.org/10.1007/978-3-658-03371-2_21

23. Strackx, R., Piessens, F.: The Heisenberg defense: proactively defending SGX enclaves against page-table-based side-channel attacks. arXiv preprint arXiv:1712.08519, December 2017

24. Van Bulck, J., Piessens, F., Strackx, R.: SGX-step: a practical attack framework for precise enclave execution control. In: Proceedings of the 2nd Workshop on System Software for Trusted Execution, SysTEX 2017, pp. 4:1–4:6. ACM (2017)

25. Van Bulck, J., Weichbrodt, N., Kapitza, R., Piessens, F., Strackx, R.: Telling your secrets without page faults: stealthy page table-based attacks on enclaved execution. In: Proceedings of the 26th USENIX Security Symposium. USENIX Association (2017)

26. Wang, W., Chen, G., Pan, X., Zhang, Y., Wang, X., Bindschaedler, V., Tang, H., Gunter, C.A.: Leaky cauldron on the dark land: understanding memory side-channel hazards in SGX. In: Proceedings of the 2017 ACM SIGSAC Conference on Computer and Communications Security, CCS 2017, pp. 2421–2434. ACM, New York (2017)

27. Xu, Y., Cui, W., Peinado, M.: Controlled-channel attacks: deterministic side channels for untrusted operating systems. In: 2015 IEEE Symposium on Security and Privacy (SP), pp. 640–656. IEEE (2015)

One Leak Is Enough to Expose Them All
From a WebRTC IP Leak to Web-Based Network Scanning

Mohammadreza Hazhirpasand$^{(\boxtimes)}$ and Mohammad Ghafari

Software Composition Group, University of Bern, Bern, Switzerland
{mhhazhirpasand,ghafari}@inf.unibe.ch

Abstract. WebRTC provides browsers and mobile apps with rich real-time communications capabilities, without the need for further software components. Recently, however, it has been shown that WebRTC can be triggered to fingerprint a web visitor, which may compromise the user's privacy. We evaluate the feasibility of exploiting a WebRTC IP leak to scan a user's private network ports and IP addresses from outside their local network. We propose a web-based network scanner that is both browser- and network-independent, and performs nearly as well as system-based scanners. We experiment with various popular mobile and desktop browsers on several platforms and show that adversaries not only can exploit WebRTC to identify the real user identity behind a web request, but also can retrieve sensitive information about the user's network infrastructure. We discuss the potential security and privacy consequences of this issue and present a browser extension that we developed to inform the user about the prospect of suspicious activities.

Keywords: Web-based network scanner · IP leak · Browser security

1 Introduction

Web browsers are amongst the most widely-used software applications to search and explore the Internet. A web browser is not just a container for web pages, but over the last few years it has been increasingly used for building cross-platform and hybrid apps in handheld devices. As a consequence, this common gateway to the Internet has been increasingly targeted by adversaries, and web-based attacks are becoming increasingly common [1].

Although modern browsers incorporate various protection techniques to achieve strong security [2], improvements in the features of these software applications may nevertheless compromise user privacy and introduce new security vulnerabilities [3]. In particular, the advent of HTML5 and CSS3 not only enables the construction of more diverse and powerful web sites and applications, but also brings on more risks especially to personal web privacy. For instance, the Canvas API enables the creation of animations and graphics in the web environment, but also facilitates the tracking of the user's browser and operating system due to different image processing engine and fonts settings [4]. The Geolocation API provides the physical location of a user, thereby potentially compromising the user's privacy [5]. In general, HTML5 facilitates web browser fingerprinting wherein one collects various pieces of information to distinguish a user from the general flow of those who surf the Internet.

In this paper we focus on the risk posed by WebRTC, a set of HTML5 APIs that enable real-time communication over peer-to-peer connections, *e.g.*, in-browser calling and video conferencing. Previous research has shown that WebRTC leaks a web visitor's real identity even behind a VPN [6]. We build on the state of the art, and examine the extent to which this issue could jeopardize the security and privacy of internal members of a network. We propose a web-based network scanner that exploits the WebRTC IP leak to collect the network information. Unlike existing Javascript scanners that are often imprecise due to several assumptions about the network and browsers, our proposed scanner is both browser- and network-independent. It employs a few heuristics such as predicting a port status based upon the round-trip delay time, and reducing the scan time by using a pop-up window, *etc.*

We conduct various experiments in a private network of 20 active nodes. The network is running at 100 Mbp speed, and a FortiGate Unified Threat Management (UTM) protects the network from outside threats. We assess the IP leak in the latest versions of browsers such as Google Chrome, Mozilla Firefox, and Opera, and in various desktop and mobile operating systems. We also compare the performance of our web-based scanner with that of several system-based scanners.

We found that except on iOS, major browsers like Firefox and Chrome are subject to the WebRTC leakage issue regardless of the underlying operating system. In our experiment, Safari on Mac, and Microsoft Edge on Windows were the only browsers that support WebRTC but do not leak the IP address, and iOS was the only operating system that did not suffer from this issue in any of the tested browsers. Through our scanning approach we identified a great number of active hosts and open ports in a test network. For instance, within about 30 s we could scan a complete IP range and discover all active nodes, as well flag those whose `http` ports were open. Once we identified active nodes, within 23 s we could scan 7 open ports that disclose various network services and running applications in this private network. We acknowledge that our web-based scanner performs almost as fast and precisely as system-based scanners.

Consequently, WebRTC information leakage does not pose a threat only for a web visitor but also all other members in her network, and we conclude that the privacy risk imposed by WebRTC could be considered high. We developed a browser extension that shields Google Chrome and Mozila FireFox against the WebRTC IP leak without compromising its features and applications.

In the remainder of this paper, Sect. 2 presents some background and attack vectors through which an adversary can exploit WebRTC IP leakage. Section 3 explains our web-based port scanning approach, followed by our experiment and the obtained results in Sect. 4. Section 5 illustrates a few attacks that we could run against nodes in a private network, and demonstrates a browser extension that we developed for protecting against such attacks. Section 6 presents an overview of the research most relevant to this work, and finally Sect. 7 concludes the paper.

2   Background

Using WebRTC every connected device, whether it is a computer, tablet, televisions, or smart gadget, can become a communication device without the installation of any third-party plug-ins. WebRTC is free, open source, and easy to use, and as of this writing, most browsers on different platforms from a desktop computer to a mobile device support WebRTC. Its broad adoption by many applications such as Google Hangouts, Facebook Messenger, Whatsapp, and Firefox Hello makes it hard for users to disable this feature [7]. Three HTML5 APIs, namely getusermedia, rtcpeerconnection, and rtcdatachannel, comprise the main part of WebRTC. To initiate a WebRTC application, browsers will request the user to grant permission to use WebRTC, and otherwise, the application would not run. This improves a user's privacy to ensure that their camera or microphone is not accessed from an untrusted web site.

Getting the private IP address of a website visitor used to be an arduous task especially as long as an adversary does not have physical access to the visitor's network, and the visitor uses TOR-like browsers, or is behind a VPN or an HTTP proxy. However, a web session in a WebRTC-powered browser may disclose critical network information without notice to an adversary even when the aforementioned privacy protection mechanisms are in place [8]. In effect, WebRTC needs to find the best path between two nodes. When establishing a peer-to-peer connection between two nodes, the private IP address of the user can be extracted with Javascript, from a Session Description Protocol (SDP) object. Consequently, WebRTC information leakage allows an adversary to silently identify the real IP address of a web visitor. This enables adversaries to scan open ports on her computer, collect information about running services and applications, and exploit a vulnerability in these programs to undertake an attack.

The WebRTC leakage issue is very similar to a recent information leakage discovered in Hotspot Shield, one of the most popular VPN providers with half a billion users.[1] First, they disclose some information regarding the network interfaces of a user. Second, both VPNs and proxies fail to protect the real IP address of the user. Third, the aforementioned information leaks without requiring any user permission. On the other hand, WebRTC as a part of HTML5 runs on nearly all major browsers on different platforms, and its privacy and security issues threaten a significantly large number of users in the globe.

There are at least three main attack vectors through which an adversary can attack a web client, and retrieve information from the victim. A seemingly legitimate but *malicious website* can include a malicious script in a web response

---

[1] https://nvd.nist.gov/vuln/detail/CVE-2018-6460.

to the client and wait for the results. In a *man-in-the-middle* attack, an adversary secretly relays and possibly injects a script into the communication between two parties, and collects the scan results. In a *cross-site scripting* attack, lack of rigorous input validation allows an adversary to inject malicious scripts into otherwise benign and trusted websites.

3   Port Scanning

This section explains our approach using WebRTC IP leakage issue to scan private nodes within a network. It is developed in Javascript and is browser-independent.

Once the script starts to execute, it checks whether a target browser supports WebRTC or not. If not, some basic information such as the browser's user agent string, as well as the public IP address will be returned, and the execution process will terminate. Otherwise, if the acquired IP falls within the ranges of private IPv4 address spaces, we proceed with port scanning.

We adopt a scanning heuristic based on timing. Through several experiments in different networks we learned that examining the round-trip delay time (RTT) within a private network could be used to estimate the status of a node in the network. We collected the elapsed time and the response message to various connection requests in a network from the browser's console. We observed that the timing is pretty much the same in various browsers, yet depends on the network latency, which is not known a priori. On the other hand, we observed that within each network the timings fall into three time windows that we can associate with open port, refused connection, and timeout. An open port indicates that the node is active and has a running service on the queried port. When a firewall refuses the connection or the port is closed, a connection refused response is expected. This message implies that the queried node (*i.e.*, the IP address) exists in the network, whereas a timeout response means that there is no such node in the network. Such messages only appear in the browser's console and, for security and privacy reasons, Javascript cannot access them. Nevertheless, we consistently observed that the response to a successful connection (*i.e.*, open port) is received earlier than a refused connection, and always a timeout is received much later than the other two. We therefore propose to cluster the initial scanning results based on their timings to determine a reliable threshold for the status of a request in a private network.

We applied a clustering heuristic that works as follows. First, we sort the data points (*i.e.*, scanning results) in ascending order, and store the result in a set. Next, we compute the absolute distance between every two consecutive data points, and store them in another set. The top three values in the latter set present the three significant changes in the data. Therefore, the data points in the first set whose indices correspond to the indices of the top three values in the other set indicate the boundaries of the clusters, respectively.

The clustering heuristic is implemented in Javascript and runs only once on the client side to automatically guide the scanning in each network. Alternatively, the timings can be plotted on the server side and the adversary can manually set the proper boundary of each cluster.

We could therefore deduce the timing thresholds based on each cluster. For instance, Table 1 shows the obtained clusters in a full range IP scan for http ports within our test network. If the response time in our network is less than 500 ms, we assume the expected port is open. In case of a refused connection, a response is expected in between 700 to 1400 ms. A response timeout usually takes much longer (*i.e.*, on average above 18 s).

Table 1. The time span thresholds in ms, computed only for our network

Open port	Refused connection	Timeout
<500	700 ≪ 1400	18000<

Making a connection request is feasible via an Image tag, a WebSocket request or an XMLHttpRequest (XHR). The first method uses an <img> tag in order to load a hypothetical picture from a remote location (*i.e.*, a node in the private network). We assume the expected port is open, only if the request fires the onload or the onerror events in the expected threshold. The second method uses the Websocket API, which enables interaction between a browser and a node in the network with lower overhead than http. In this method, we measure the timing as long as the the connection status is on the connecting state (*i.e.*, the readyState attribute is 0). The third method uses XHR, and we check the value of statusText attribute. Due to the restriction of the same-origin policy this value is error if there is a response from the remote location. Otherwise, In XHR a timeout response often takes 21 s and therefore we abort the connection if it takes more than the maximum threshold of interest (*i.e.*, 1400 ms).

The time required for port scanning is critical as a web session on a particular website may be short. We decreased the scanning time by scanning in parallel. In particular, we employed the popup window technique to split the number of IPs to scan between the main window and a very small popup window that we open in the rightmost corner of the screen and behind the main window. Such parallelism improves the scanning time up to 44% in total.[2] Moreover, when several clients within the same network are infected, we distribute the scanning amongst these nodes and aggregate the results in the end.

The scanning continues till it completes or as long as the victim is navigating within the infected page. We periodically persist the scanning results to local storage on the victim's browser to minimise data loss in circumstances where the scanning cannot proceed (*e.g.*, when the victim navigates to a different website, or closes the browser). Moreover, we realised when the infected tab is not active or when a browser is minimized, the scanner may not perform as expected due

---

[2] We send a new request every 200 ms.

to "background timer throttling" policies. In fact, in such circumstances both Chrome and Firefox enforce a timer task to run at most every 1000 ms.[3] We resume an incomplete scan once it is feasible (*e.g.*, when the victim visits the page again), and finally collect the network information.

4   Experiment

In this section, we conducted an experiment to find the IP address of a website visitor, and scanned nodes within the visitor's network. The visitor's network is a test lab designed to evaluate the performance of our port scanner. We simulated a malicious website by injecting a script (*i.e.*, our scanner) into the comment section of a website, so that when a visitor clicks on the "show comments" button, the script will run on the visitor's private network. We collected the private network information of the website's visitors in our experiment, and ran a few attacks against the internal nodes in the network.

We further evaluated the generalizability of our network scanning approach by carrying out another experiment in a wireless network with which we were not familiar in advance.

4.1   Setup

Table 2 presents an overview of 20 active machines in our first experimental network. We manually added Android and iOS devices to this network for experimentation purposes. The whole network is protected by a FortiGate Unified Threat Management (UTM) firewall with a default configuration. Five Windows machines in the network are also protected by Kaspersky products, and the remaining ones are equipped only with the default firewall installed on each machine.

Table 2. Test lab nodes and their open ports

OS	No of machines	Open ports
Windows	14	80,443,445,3306,110,1433,25,43,7,139,902
Linux	3	80,443,8080,22
MacOS	1	21,22
Android	1	2221
iOS	1	5612

We examined the WebRTC information leakage issue in the latest versions of major browsers in each operating system. In particular, we tested the Google Chrome, Chromium, Mozilla Firefox, Internet Explorer, Microsoft Edge, Safari,

---

[3] https://developers.google.com/web/updates/2017/03/background_tabs.

Samsung Internet, and Opera browsers. We performed two tests; in the first test the scan goes from IP address 1 to 254 to identify active nodes in general, and in particular to flag web servers in the victim's private network. In the second test we collect more information about the target network by scanning a broader range of ports only on the active nodes that were identified in the previous test. Generally, scanning the whole range of ports could be time-consuming and users do not spend more than several minutes on a typical web page. Moreover, adversaries usually look for ports that are often associated to particular software systems that they can exploit. Therefore, it is common to scan only a number of ports on a victim's machine. Table 3 presents the list of ports that we scan in each node in the second experiment. We selected these ports randomly from the entire list of open ports in the network.

Table 3. The open ports in the target network

Port	Description
3306	MySQL database system
1433	Microsoft SQL Server database management system (MSSQL) server
8080	Apache Tomcat
902	VMware ESXi
2221	WiFi FTP Server android application
445	Windows shares
80	Hypertext Transfer Protocol (HTTP)

In another experiment, we also ran the same two tests via a browser connected to the wireless network. In both experiments we use our clustering heuristic which automatically determines the status of a network request. We compare our results with three popular IP/Port scanning software tools, namely Angry IP Scanner[4], Advanced IP Scanner[5], and Advanced Port Scanner[6]. We set http port, banner grabber, and ping options in the first test. We repeat each test five times to mitigate bias in the measured performance.

There exist a few security tools that employ WebRTC to get the internal IP addresses of a victim's network. For instance, a tool named BeEF (http:// beefproject.com) has a feature called "Get Internal IP Address", however, our experiment with this tool showed that it suffers from a large number of false positives so that, in the interest of space, we do not discuss it in this paper.

4.2   Result

Table 4 presents a list of popular browsers that were examined for the WebRTC private IP leak. We found that except on iOS, major browsers like Firefox and

---

[4] http://angryip.org.

[5] http://www.advanced-ip-scanner.com.

[6] https://www.advanced-port-scanner.com.

Chrome are subject to the WebRTC private IP leak regardless of the underlying operating system. In our experiment, Safari on Mac, and Microsoft Edge on Windows were the only browsers that support WebRTC but do not leak the IP address, and iOS was the only operating system that did not suffer from this issue in any of the tested browsers.

Further investigation is needed into the implementation of these browsers to uncover the reason they do not leak the private IP address of a user.

Table 4. The state of WebRTC support in major browsers

Browser	Version	OS	WebRCT	Private IP Leak
Google Chrome	63	Windows	Yes	Yes
Mozilla Firefox	57	Windows	Yes	Yes
Internet Explorer	11	Windows	No	No
Microsoft Edge	16	Windows	Yes	No
Opera	49	Windows	Yes	Yes
Mozilla Firefox	54	Android	Yes	Yes
Google Chrome	59	Android	Yes	Yes
Opera Mini	32	Android	No	No
Samsung Browser	6.2	Android	Yes	Yes
Safari	11	Mac	Yes	No
Google Chrome	63	Mac	Yes	Yes
Mozilla Firefox	58	Mac	Yes	Yes
Safari	10	iOS	Yes	No
Google Chrome	64	iOS	Yes	No
Mozilla Firefox	10	iOS	Yes	No
Opera Mini	16	iOS	No	No
Mozilla Firefox	51	Ubuntu	Yes	Yes
Chromium	35	Ubuntu	Yes	Yes
Opera	51	Ubuntu	Yes	Yes
Google Chrome	64	Ubuntu	Yes	Yes

We successfully identified 20 active nodes and flagged 8 whose http ports were open in the first experiment. The average time to scan a complete range in all three methods in the main window of a browser is around 55 s. When the scanning is also assigned to a popup window the time significantly decreases to about 31 s (*i.e.*, 44% improvement).[7] We realised that the IMG tag approach may make the victim aware of ongoing suspicious activities. For example, in our experiment Firefox shows the IP addresses that are being loaded in the status bar.

---

[7] Distributing the work amongst more popup windows could improve the speed, but the risk that they will be noticed by the user increases as well.

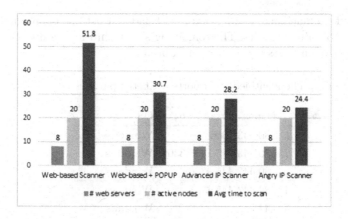

Fig. 1. The performance of scanners in the first test, first experiment

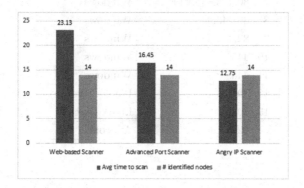

Fig. 2. The comparison of scanners in the second test, first experiment

Figure 1 presents a comparison of our web-based scanner with two state-of-the-art network scanner tools. All the scanners are successful at identifying the nodes in the network. System-based scanners perform faster than our web-based scanner but only slightly faster when a popup window is employed. Moreover, system-based scanners have a higher privilege to scan all ports, perform ICMP requests, and use multi-threaded features. In contrast, in this experiment we found that due to security concerns Javascript is not allowed to communicate with all ports. In fact, out of 65535 ports, Javascript was banned from scanning 59 ports. These ports are listed in Table 8 in the Appendix. In addition, the performance of our scanner depends on the system resources that are allocated to the infected tab in a browser, as discussed in Sect. 3.

Figure 2 illustrates the results of the second test in which we scanned several ports listed in Table 3. The average time for scanning dropped significantly in all methods as we only scanned the active nodes *i.e.*, 20 machines.

Amongst 20 machines in the network, 14 had at least one open port. Table 5 presents the obtained results. The remaining six machines were not identified as none of their open ports were listed in Table 3.

Table 5. The identified open ports w.r.t. the ports listed in Table 3

	Open ports	OS
1	80,443,3306	Windows
2	80,443,445,1433,3306	Windows
3	80,443,445,3306	Windows
4	80,443,445	Windows
5	445	Windows
6	902	Windows
7	80,443,445,3306	Windows
8	80,443,445	Windows
9	80,443,445	Windows
10	445	Windows
11	445	Windows
12	80,443	Linux (Ubuntu)
13	8080	Linux (Arch)
14	2221	Android

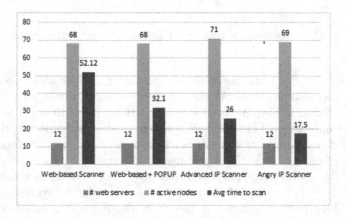

Fig. 3. The performance of scanners in the first test, second experiment

In the following, we briefly discuss the results obtained in the second experiment within a wireless network. According to Fig. 3, the performance of scanners in the first test is consistent with our findings in the previous experiment, though the Angry IP Scanner has performed slightly better than before. We found the number of identified active nodes varies a bit as few clients connected or disconnected to the network during our experiment. In the second test we examined the status of the ports in Table 3, and amongst 68 active nodes we found 17 nodes with open ports (see Fig. 4). It is worth mentioning that the scan completion in our web-based scanner took much longer than the second test in the first experiment as there were about five times as many nodes, and we did not employ any parallelism.

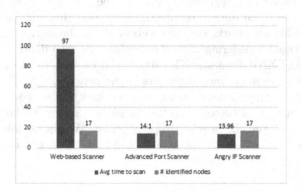

Fig. 4. The comparison of scanners in the second test, second experiment

Therefore, the obtained results in our experiments confirm that our approach for network scanning performs reliably and independent of the underlying network.

4.3 Threats to Validity

The firewall in our test lab was set up with its default configuration, and did not prevent port scanning. In fact, perimeter firewalls often control the flow of network traffic entering or leaving an organization, whereas the origin of scanning is an internal node, and this bypasses many existing rules on firewall systems. Moreover, finding the right timing thresholds is a non-trivial task due to the network congestion, in-place firewall systems, and various policies like timing and resource allocation in browsers. Hence, a node whose response time takes longer than the selected thresholds may mistakenly be assumed to be unavailable. We mitigated this threat by scanning only when the infected tab is the active tab in a browser, and employing a clustering technique to predict a port status. Finally, our experiment was limited to IPv4 scanning and the obtained results may not generalise to IPv6.

5 Risks and Countermeasures

Besides serious privacy concerns that a remote network scanning imposes, the collected information facilitates a number of attacks against the nodes in a network. In this section, we briefly mention a few attacks that we conducted, and thereafter, we present our simple approach, implemented as a browser extension, to protect against such attacks.

5.1 Attacks

We run a Denial of Service (DoS) attack against a web server in the network through the browser of a legitimate client in the network. This is interesting as security devices often underestimate the likelihood that such an attack may happen from inside a network. We use a web worker in Javascript, running in the background without interfering with the user interface, to flood the target web server with many XHR requests. The attack can be turned into a Distributed DoS attack if we can infect more browsers in the network.

Table 6 presents the maximum number of requests that we could send within one minute from various browsers to the target web server, without impacting the user experience and the browser responsiveness. We also measured the page load before and at the time of the attack, and found that it increases by 20% delay when running the attack.

Table 6. Number of requests from each browser during a DoS attack

Browser	Platform	Requests in one minute
Google Chrome	Windows	5820
Mozilla Firefox	Windows	5210
Opera	Windows	5442
Mozilla Firefox	Linux (Ubuntu)	3266
Google Chrome	Linux (Ubuntu)	4085
Mozilla Firefox	Android	4231
Google Chrome	Android	3005
Opera Mini	Android	3845

Next, we run a brute-force attack to mine sensitive files and directories from web servers. We selected 600 common paths, and measured the performance when targeting one, three, and five web servers. We checked the availability of a remote path via JSONP as it is able to establish GET requests without the restriction of the same-origin policy. In particular, JSONP expects a response only in JSON format, otherwise if the path exists it returns a `parsererror` message, and if it does not exist it returns an `error` message. Table 7 presents the obtained results.

Internal web applications often lack spam protection mechanism like Captcha code for authentication. Therefore, we can brute-force the login page in such applications. We speculated on the type of web applications installed on each web server based on the identified paths. In one case where we could identify the

Table 7. The path brute-force results in one minute

No of web servers	Examined paths	Identified paths
1	600	12
3	200	15
5	120	18

presence of a protected directory of image files, we remotely brute forced 1000 common passwords within 80 s. In particular, in each request we sent credentials as a POST request to the login page through a hidden `iframe` element within the infected page. As we are aware of a protected image, we load the image using the `IMG` tag. In case the image loads successfully, it means the session is set for the visitor, and the last tried password is correct.

5.2 WebRTC IP Leak Guard

The easiest way to shield against a WebRTC IP leak is to disable it in the browser. Extensions like WebRTC Block and WebRTC Control offer this possibility to a browser, however the risk is that users may not remember to disable WebRTC after each use. There exist a couple of browser extensions like WebRTC Leak Prevent, and WebRTC Network Limiter that allow only the use of public IP in WebRTC. Nevertheless, not all browsers support this feature as it may inhibit the adoption of many useful applications for which WebRTC is proposed.

We have developed a browser extension for Google Chrome and Mozilla Firefox that monitors the network information, and warns about requests that may be related to scanning and attacking internal nodes within a network. In particular, it records the connections destined to local IP addresses, and once the number of such connections exceeds a certain configurable threshold, the extension will notify the user of a suspicious activity. The extension has also a whitelist feature that contains addresses for Intranet applications and services that will not be monitored.

6 Related Work

In this section we review related work that studies WebRTC from a security and privacy standpoint. Recent research has highlighted the role of choosing the right browser and VPN in order to avoid WebRTC leakage [6]. The author found that TorGuard is the least privacy-compromising VPN service, while VyprVPN and ExpressVPN failed to prevent WebRTC IP leaks. Similar to our findings, he found Safari to be the most privacy-preserving browser. In a study of the top one million sites on Alexa [9], the authors found WebRTC being used to discover local IP addresses without user interaction on 715 sites, and mainly for tracking.

In a research on web device fingerprinting [8], the authors classified 29 browser-based device fingerprinting techniques in which WebRTC is graded as a medium-level threat. A study of the fingerprintability of browsers found that WebRTC exposes identical device IDs of hardware components like webcam, microphone and speaker across multiple browsers when visiting a particular website [10]. While the aforementioned studies mostly focused on WebRTC IP leakage for user fingerprinting, Reiter and Marsalek [11] used WebRTC for conducting a couple of attacks like DDoS against a remote peer in the network. They also proposed the possibility of targeting internal nodes within a network by using a Javascript network scanner, named jslanscanner.[8] However, our investigation reveals that this scanner is bound to identify routers within a network by probing their well-known default IP addresses and under the assumption that some expected image files are available on these routers. Our experiments showed that this scanner produces a very large number of false positives due to its predefined threshold (*i.e.*, 15 s) for open ports, which varies in miscellaneous circumstances discussed earlier in Sect. 3.

To sum up, previous work mainly mentioned WebRTC information leaks, but their experiments were mostly limited to the choice of VPNs and browsers. Moreover, scanner tools like BeEF that use WebRTC suffer from a large number of false positives. We conjecture that this is due to their failure in adapting the appropriate timing with respect to a target network.

7   Conclusion

We focus on exploiting the WebRTC IP leakage issue for collecting critical information about a private network. In particular, we propose a web-based scanner that leverages this IP leakage to infiltrate a private network, and to discover active nodes and their open ports. The proposed scanner adopts a simple clustering algorithm to bypass the restrictions of previous web-based scanners that need to decide about the network latency a priory.

We compare our approach with state-of-the-art network scanners. Regardless of 59 ports that are banned from being scanned in Javascript, our web-based scanner performs only slightly slower than the system-based scanners. We briefly discuss several security implications of this issue, and introduce a browser extension that we developed for Chrome and Firefox for informing the user about such dubious activities in these browsers.

Acknowledgments. We appreciate the valuable feedback from Prof. Oscar Nierstrasz, as well as all parties who kindly allowed us to carry out several tests in their private networks. We gratefully acknowledge the funding of the Swiss National Science Foundations for the project "Agile Software Analysis" (SNF project No. 200020_162352, Jan 1, 2016–Dec. 30, 2018) (http://p3.snf.ch/Project-162352). We also thank CHOOSE, the Swiss Group for Original and Outside-the-box Software Engineering of the Swiss Informatics Society, for its financial contribution to the presentation of this paper.

---

[8] https://code.google.com/archive/p/jslanscanner/.

Appendix

Table 8. The 59 ports that were banned for scanning via Javascript

Port	Assignment description	Port	Assignment description
0	Reserved	139	NETBIOS Session Service
1	TCP Port Service Multiplexer	143	Internet Message Access Protocol
7	Echo	179	Border Gateway Protocol - BGP
9	Discard	389	Lightweight Directory Access Protocol
11	Active Users	465	URL Rendezvous Directory for SSM - Message Submission over TLS protocol
13	Daytime	512	remote process execution; authentication performed using passwords and UNIX login names
15	Unassigned	513	automatic authentication performed based on priviledged port numbers
17	Quote of the Day	514	cmd like exec, but automatic authentication is performed as for login server
19	Character Generator	515	spooler
20	File Transfer [Default Data]	526	newdate
21	File Transfer Protocol [Control]	530	rpc
22	The Secure Shell (SSH) Protocol	531	chat
23	Telnet	532	readnews
25	Simple Mail Transfer	540	uucpd
37	Time	556	rfs server
42	Host Name Server	563	nntp protocol over TLS/SSL (was snntp)
43	Who Is	587	Message Submission
53	Domain Name Server	601	Reliable Syslog Service
77	any private RJE service	636	ldap protocol over TLS/SSL (was sldap)
79	Finger	993	IMAP over TLS protocol
87	any private terminal link	995	POP3 over TLS protocol
95	SUPDUP	2049	Network File System - Sun Microsystems
101	NIC Host Name Server	4045	Network Paging Protocol
102	ISO-TSAP Class 0	6000	X Window System
103	Genesis Point-to-Point Trans Net		
104	ACRNEMA Digital Imag. & Comm. 300		
109	Post Office Protocol - Version 2		
110	Post Office Protocol - Version 3		
111	SUN Remote Procedure Call		
113	Authentication Service		
115	Simple File Transfer Protocol		
117	UUCP Path Service		
119	Network News Transfer Protocol		
123	Network Time Protocol		
135	DCE endpoint resolution		

References

1. Zhang, M., Lu, S., Xu, B.: An anomaly detection method based on multi-models to detect web attacks. In: Computational Intelligence and Design, pp. 404–409, December 2017
2. Rogowski, R., Morton, M., Li, F., Monrose, F., Snow, K.Z., Polychronakis, M.: Revisiting browser security in the modern era: new data-only attacks and defenses. In: Proceedings - 2nd IEEE European Symposium on Security and Privacy, EuroS and P 2017, pp. 366–381 (2017)
3. Luangmaneerote, S., Zaluska, E., Carr, L.: Inhibiting browser fingerprinting and tracking. In: Proceedings - 3rd IEEE International Conference on Big Data Security on Cloud, BigDataSecurity 2017, 3rd IEEE International Conference on High Performance and Smart Computing, HPSC 2017 and 2nd IEEE International Conference on Intelligent Data and Securit, pp. 63–68 (2017)
4. Mowery, K., Shacham, H.: Pixel perfect: fingerprinting Canvas in HTML5. In: Web 2.0 Security & Privacy (W2SP), vol. 20, pp. 1–12 (2012)
5. Yoon, S., Jung, J., Kim, H.: Attacks on web browsers with HTML5. In: 2015 10th International Conference for Internet Technology and Secured Transactions, ICITST 2015, pp. 193–197 (2016)
6. Al-Fannah, N.M.: One leak will sink a ship: WebRTC IP address leaks, pp. 1–12. arXiv preprint arXiv:1709.05395 (2017)
7. Cox, J.H., Clark, R., Owen, H.: Leveraging SDN and WebRTC for rogue access point security. IEEE Trans. Netw. Serv. Manag. **14**(3), 756–770 (2017)
8. Alaca, F., van Oorschot, P.C.: Device fingerprinting for augmenting web authentication. In: Proceedings of the 32nd Annual Conference on Computer Security Applications - ACSAC 2016, pp. 289–301 (2016)
9. Englehardt, S., Narayanan, A.: Online tracking: a 1-million-site measurement and analysis. In: Proceedings of the 2016 ACM SIGSAC Conference on Computer and Communications Security - CCS 2016, no. 1, pp. 1388–1401 (2016)
10. Al-Fannah, N.M., Li, W.: Not all browsers are created equal: comparing web browser fingerprintability. In: Obana, S., Chida, K. (eds.) IWSEC 2017. LNCS, vol. 10418, pp. 105–120. Springer, Cham (2017). https://doi.org/10.1007/978-3-319-64200-0_7
11. Reiter, A., Marsalek, A.: WebRTC: your privacy is at risk. In: Proceedings of the Symposium on Applied Computing - SAC 2017, pp. 664–669 (2017, in Press)

PrivacyMeter: Designing and Developing a Privacy-Preserving Browser Extension

Oleksii Starov$^{(\boxtimes)}$ and Nick Nikiforakis

Stony Brook University, Stony Brook,
NY 11794, USA
{ostarov,nick}@cs.stonybrook.edu

Abstract. Anti-tracking browser extensions are popular among web users since they provide them with the ability to limit the number of trackers who get to learn about their browsing habits. These extensions however are limited in that they ignore other privacy signals, such as, the presence of a privacy policy, use of HTTPS, or presence of insecure web forms that can leak PII. To effectively inform users about the privacy consequences of visiting particular websites, we design, implement, and evaluate PRIVACYMETER, a browser extension that, on-the-fly, computes a relative privacy score for any website that a user is visiting. This score is computed based on each website's privacy practices and how these compare to the privacy practices of other pre-analyzed websites. We report on the development of PRIVACYMETER with respect to the requirements for coverage of privacy practices, accuracy of measurement, and low performance overhead. We show how relative privacy scores help in interpreting results as different categories of websites have different standards across the monitored privacy parameters. Finally, we discuss the power of crowdsourcing for privacy research, and the existing challenges of properly incorporating crowdsourcing in a way that protects user anonymity while allowing the service to defend against malicious clients.

1 Introduction

The modern web is home to many online services that request and handle sensitive private information from their users. For example, most of the popular websites require personal information to create an account, including one's email address, name, and date of birth, or even ask users to provide similar information in order to just submit a contact form. Unfortunately, this sensitive data is not always collected and handled in the most confidential and secure way possible. Previous research has shown how websites may leak user information, either due to poor programming practices [6,13,18,26], or through the intentional outsourcing of functionality to third-party services [6,26]. One of the most intrusive

---

The stamp on the top of this paper refers to an approval process conducted by the ESSoS Artifact Evaluation Committee.

© Springer International Publishing AG, part of Springer Nature 2018
M. Payer et al. (Eds.): ESSoS 2018, LNCS 10953, pp. 77–95, 2018.
https://doi.org/10.1007/978-3-319-94496-8_6

scenarios is the leakage of a user's personally identifiable information (PII) to web trackers, which can then match it with existing pseudonymous user identifiers (such as cookies and browser/device fingerprints) and thus deanonymize the user across browsing sessions and websites.

Despite the magnitude of this problem, users today have few, if any, options, for protecting their PII against accidental and intentional leakage. Generic anti-tracking extensions, such as Ghostery [9], Disconnect [8], and uBlock Origin [29] or other ad blockers [4,5,28], operate solely using manually-curated blacklists which, due to their reactive nature, are destined to be always out of date [19]. Moreover, these anti-tracking extensions only account for domains belonging to tracking companies and thus cannot account for non-tracking-related third-party domains which happen to receive a user's PII due to the poor programming practices of the first-party website with which the user interacts. In addition, current anti-tracking extensions are rather myopic in the sense that they only care about the third-party trackers available on a webpage, but ignore other signals (such as the presence of a privacy policy, or the use of HTTPS) which are directly correlated with the confidentiality of user data. Finally, next to the lack of technology, websites are becoming more and more hostile towards any kind of client-side tracking-blocking tools forcing users to whitelist them before they can get access to their content [11,12,20], taking away what little control users had regained.

As such, the sole focus on blocking trackers may not be sufficient to preserve the privacy of web users, and more attention should be given to improve their overall awareness about the privacy-related consequences of visiting any given website. For example, in addition to a list of detected trackers, a privacy-preserving browser extension can convey to non-technical users, which of those trackers pose a serious threat to their privacy—and therefore must be blocked—and which are reliable and can be allowed. Similarly, such a tool should take into account and evaluate as many additional privacy practices on a website as possible, in order to provide user with a complete picture of the expected privacy guarantees.

To effectively inform users about the privacy consequences of visiting particular websites, we propose, design, implement, and evaluate PRIVACYMETER, a browser extension that, on-the-fly, computes a relative privacy score for any website that a user is visiting. This score is computed based on each website's privacy practices (e.g., reputation of trackers, amount of third-party content or presence of insecure "leaky" web forms) and how these compare to the privacy practices of other pre-analyzed websites. In addition to the overall risk score, PRIVACYMETER also provides users with contextual information about the discovered privacy issues (e.g., "many aggressive trackers", or "many inputs are submitted to third parties"), and what actions are advised. This is a clear departure from virtually all other available browser extensions which merely inform the user about the total number of trackers on any given page and assume that the user is somehow capable of using this information in a constructive manner.

In this paper we provide details on the design and development of PRIVACYMETER, including the covered privacy practices and encountered implementation challenges, as well as additional envisioned features, which may be implemented in later versions. Development of such a privacy-preserving browser extension is not trivial as each privacy-related feature must be reliably and accurately retrieved, the overall privacy scores calculated in the same fashion over all of the websites in order to guarantee their comparability, and the results must be presented on time with low performance overhead. At the same time, there is another level of challenges, which lie in the research and crowdsourcing nature of the tool.

The key contributions of this paper are as follows:

– We describe our case study of implementing a complex privacy-preserving browser extension, PRIVACYMETER, which provides a real-time privacy quantification for the web, and has strong requirements for coverage, accuracy, and performance.
– We identify and group important privacy features of websites in order to design an informative user interface, which combines comparable privacy values with immediate unconditional warnings.
– We show how relative privacy score helps in improving the privacy awareness as different categories of websites have different privacy standards across the monitored privacy parameters.
– We measure the performance overhead from PRIVACYMETER and compare it to Ghostery, a state-of-the-art commercial anti-tracking extension.
– We describe the benefits of crowdsourcing as a necessary feature both for the quality of PRIVACYMETER, as well as for the further research benefits. At the same time, we discuss the challenges in adopting crowdsourcing in any privacy-preserving tool due to: (a) higher anonymity and transparency requirements when collecting the data; (b) potential of a polluted data from malicious clients.

2   Design and Interface

PRIVACYMETER is developed as a browser extension which, upon installation, enhances each tab of a web browser with new privacy-related information. Whenever a user visits a new website, PRIVACYMETER computes a numerical privacy score for that website, which is an overall count of detected privacy issues, and warns the user about privacy risks by changing the color of its icon from green to yellow or red depending on the severity of the identified risks. Each issue can be a *definite* privacy risk (e.g., if a web page does not use HTTPS or does not have a privacy policy), or a *potential* relative privacy risk (e.g., if a web page has 17% more third-party trackers than average for similar websites). PRIVACYMETER augments, in a non-intrusive fashion, the UI of the browser to add the computed number of privacy issues to its icon in the right top corner of the URL bar, and gives users the ability to find the rationale behind this score as well as advice on how to proceed by clicking it.

Figure 1a shows an example of the extension's popup with details on the discovered privacy-related issues at the money.cnn.com page. The interface consists

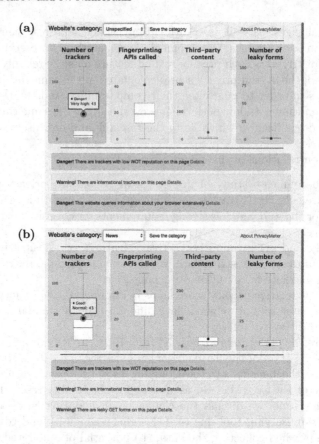

Fig. 1. UI and information provided by PRIVACYMETER on the example of visiting money.cnn.com page: (a) comparing privacy features to *any* other websites; (b) comparing privacy features to other *news* websites. (Color figure online)

of the two main parts: (1) box plots to show the relative privacy risks; (2) text warnings with definite privacy risks (or with additional details about relative risks). In both cases, we use the aforementioned three-color scheme to highlight the severity of the threat, where green is used as "safe", yellow as "potentially dangerous", and red as "dangerous" level. For instance, if the web page contains too many trackers (in comparison with other similar sites), the corresponding box plot will be colored with yellow or red. Similarly, if the page contains any number of low-reputation trackers, the corresponding message will be highlighted with red. PRIVACYMETER also gives users the ability to get additional details, whether by hovering the mouse over the particular box plot, or by clicking on each text warning.

The main functionality of PRIVACYMETER is to provide users with understandable privacy scores of the websites that they visit. To be usable, these scores must reflect the privacy practices of websites in such a way, that users intuitively understand and agree with them. As such, in order to evaluate the severity of a particular relative privacy issue we compare the value for the current web page to the mean value over other websites: if it is greater than the mean plus one standard deviation, we mark it as "potentially dangerous," and if it is greater than the mean plus two standard deviations, we mark it as a "dangerous" issue. The overall privacy score presented to a user is the number of all the privacy issues found on the page, which is colored with red if at least one of the issues falls into the "dangerous" category.

Despite our best efforts to score privacy issues in an objective way, we anticipate that a fraction of advanced users may not entirely agree with the default scoring thresholds or with the set of privacy features that comprise our privacy score. To maintain the usability of our tool, we allow users to remove some factors from the score calculation on the extension's setting page to better reflect their privacy preferences. Similarly, PRIVACYMETER provides an option to compare relative factors to median and the third quartile of a distribution instead of the mean-based comparison, as well as to change the base threat level (whether to relax it by counting considerable risks as safe, or to consider any number of trackers or leaky web forms as dangerous).

The text warnings assist users with the decision whether to limit (or stop) the browsing of a web page. For instance, when a leaky form is discovered, the corresponding message advises user to refrain from trusting the website with their PII. We decided to use box plots in addition to the text warnings with the assumption that visual information is easier and quicker to understand. Particularly, we chose box plots for the type of plot as those clearly show how a single data point compares to the overall distribution of values. We argue that with a little training, even non-technical users are able to read such visualizations faster then text explanations, and develop an intuition about relative privacy risks.

As an additional functionality, PRIVACYMETER's interface provides a control to select a category for the current website. In this case, all the relative privacy risks will be compared to other known web pages of only the selected category. For instance, Fig. 1b shows how the picture changes for money.cnn.com if we consider only news websites. Given that news sites tend to have more trackers than other types of websites (we quantify this in Sect. 3), the 43 trackers of money.cnn.com are not considered an outlier and therefore PRIVACYMETER's warnings regarding the number of trackers disappear. We argue that this ability to compare with other similar websites helps web users to translate raw numbers into the privacy expectations, i.e., to immediately gauge whether their website of interest stands out in a positive (i.e. more private than average) or negative (i.e. less private than average) direction.

Monitored Privacy Practices

To provide a representative privacy score, PRIVACYMETER must account for different privacy practices, web security vulnerabilities, and other factors on a website. As we explained above, factors which are *potential* privacy risks can be represented by comparative metrics, whereas factors which are *definite* risks are usually represented using binary values. PRIVACYMETER deploys mechanisms to test a web page against the following four main groups of privacy risks (each group has a correspond box plot on the interface in Fig. 1):

- **Third-party trackers.** To measure the potential privacy risk due to third-party trackers, we first calculate the comparative metric on how the number of trackers differs from the average number of trackers for similar websites. The result is visualized on the corresponding box plot. Second, we answer additional questions that may also correlate with the potential privacy risks, such as what is the number of trackers served from international servers. Similarly, the severity of the warning message depends on how this quantity deviates from the average but it is, by default, marked as "potentially dangerous" even if only one international tracker is present. Finally, an example of a definite privacy risk marked as "dangerous" is the presence of trackers with low reputation (according to the Web-of-Trust score [30]).

- **Fingerprinting activity.** Fingerprinting activity may correlate with intrusive tracking, either from an advanced third-party tracker or the first-party website. The privacy threat lies in the fact that fingerprinting is immune to the deletion of stateful identifiers (such as cookies) and thus harder to avoid. The main metric we calculate is a relative number of unique called APIs (as utilized by Lerner et al. [15]), which are known to be used for fingerprinting browsers and devices. The corresponding box plot visualizes the comparison with the sample distribution. In addition, we show a separate warning for the cumulative number of API calls, which may correlate with continuous fingerprinting attempts.

- **Third-party content.** If a web page is populated with third-party content, a user may be easily tricked into interacting and sharing sensitive information with parties other than the ones expected. For instance, a website may load a large number of iframes with third-party ads completely overlaying the page, or it may incorporate a third-party form widget. PRIVACYMETER answers the question on how the number of third-party widgets differs from the average for similar websites. In future versions, we can also warn about signs of visually overlapping iframes.

- **Leaky web forms.** PRIVACYMETER has ability to identify web forms that may leak entered information, such as forms implemented with HTTP GET method and thus exposing the entered values in URL and HTTP Referer headers, forms submitting without HTTPS or forms directly submitting to a third-party domain. Next to warning messages about the presence of such forms, we provide a comparison on the number of leaky forms in the corresponding box plot. The rationale for that lies in the fact that some categories of websites may include numerous unsafe search forms, or other forms that do not necessary request PII or other sensitive private information. In our current version of PRIVACYMETER, we assign a dangerous level to a leaky web form if it contains a large number of visible inputs (such as the ones used during account creation), or one or more sensitive fields (such as a password field).

In addition, PRIVACYMETER collects features that can be used as "proxies" of the level of privacy and security awareness of the website owners. For example, PRIVACYMETER checks whether a P3P privacy policy is available to the users. Even though we are fully aware that such a policy is not a guarantee of proper privacy measures, we argue that its absence is a strong negative indicator. We also detect signs of mixed HTTP/HTTPS inclusions, and out-of-date versions of web servers, which quantifies the extent to which website administrators update their software. The overall privacy score is calculated as a sum of issues found among these parameters, and users are also notified about each separate issue as shown in Fig. 1. Note that PRIVACYMETER is unique in that it goes above and beyond the measuring of standard privacy practices, by also measuring security issues which could be abused to compromise the confidentiality of a user's private information (such as a web server getting compromised and the user's data exfiltrated, because of the use of out-of-date software with known exploitable vulnerabilities).

Architectural Challenges

In the previous section, we provided a list of factors that PRIVACYMETER uses to calculate the privacy score of a website. The extension part of PRIVACYMETER is responsible for retrieving them using a combination of static and dynamic techniques, as those are allowed by modern browser-extension frameworks. Even though some of these factors can be straightforwardly detected, e.g., version of a web server or mixed HTTP/HTTPS requests, others could pose technical challenges. For instance, a privacy policy may be present in a wide range of locations (making it hard to automatically locate) and trackers may use stealthy tracking techniques to avoid being easily detected. As such, the current architecture of PRIVACYMETER's extension, shown on Fig. 2a, already includes several modules running in the contexts of extension's background script, content scripts, as well as inside the web page context. In order to identify privacy risks, each module runs a set of tests on every newly visited web page, and analyzes every new web request.

Given the goal of building a user-friendly and reliable privacy-enhancing system, we can distinguish the following three challenges in the realization of the client-side logic.

Coverage of Privacy Factors. PRIVACYMETER incorporates open source code from Adblock Plus to implement our tracker filter, and uses an up-to-date EasyPrivacy list to identify trackers. As we mentioned earlier, such blacklists, by definition, cannot guarantee detection of all trackers. Thus, PRIVACYMETER deploys another module to detect indirect signs of intrusive tracking, namely fingerprinting activity. On Fig. 2a, the FAPI monitor reports to the main score engine all the calls to fingerprinting-related APIs. In order to listen API calls from a web page, the module injects proxy code to the context of each visited web page, which intercepts more than 60 APIs of interest (e.g., navigator.plugins to attempt enumerating plugins or HTMLElement.getBoundingClientRect involved

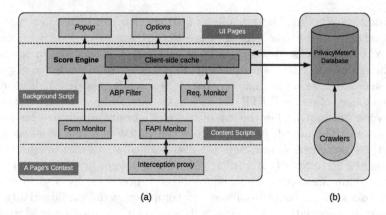

Fig. 2. PRIVACYMETER's architecture: (a) client-side modules inside browser extension; (b) server-side support with the central database and automatic crawler.

in font enumeration via JavaScript [21]). For a complete list of APIs see Appendix B.

Comparability of the Values. PRIVACYMETER compares many parameters among different websites in order to calculate a relative privacy scores. To make this comparison representative and fair, the tests must be performed in the same fashion across all the web pages. For instance, one challenge is to unify the duration of measurements as users spend different time on different websites. We can imagine a situation where a new tracking script is dynamically loaded on the page after a one-minute delay, or after a particular user action. While this does not affect the client-side functionality of the extension as the privacy score shown to the user is dynamically updated, on the back end we take into account that one URL may naturally have different measurements, and we want to record the duration of each test. Another affected factor is the fingerprinting activity, though in this case later API calls may be a legitimate result of the user's actions on a page, and should not be attributed to the tracker's script. To allow the comparison of fingerprinting APIs we decided to record fingerprinting activity only during the first five seconds on the page, assuming that the most tracking activity happens immediately after loading tracking scripts. Naturally this threshold is configurable and can be changed to fit different use cases.

Performance Side-Effects. An important requirement of PRIVACYMETER is that of low performance overhead as this directly affects the usability of the tool. As such, we use the state-of-the-art code by Adblock Plus to detect tracking requests as fast as possible, and optimize each custom monitoring module to perform less comparisons and function calls when analyzing new requests, web forms, and iframes. Moreover, we deploy the following strategies:

- **Lazy-loading and batch processing.** When a web page is loading, new trackers, web forms, iframes and API calls appear one by one. In real-time, each new item has to be processed by the corresponding PRIVACYMETER's module, and the overall privacy score has to be updated. A naive approach would be to process each item separately and immediately request a redrawing of the privacy score. Practically, this results in high performance overhead as numerous messages are generated passing between different contexts of the browser extension. Moreover, information such as a tracker's Web-of-Trust score is requested from the back-end via HTTP requests, and it can therefore be expensive to issue a separate request for each tracker. Similarly, a call to the function that provides geolocation based on a tracker's IP address is also time-consuming. As such, we decided to use batch-processing after lazy loading of new items. Technically, we launch a periodical update event which, once every 0.5 s, surveys all the modules about newly gathered information, and re-calculates the privacy issues and score. This helps to decouple the extension's UI from the score calculations, and keep it responsive to other user actions.

– **Client-side and server-side caching.** Even with batch processing, we issue at least one bulk request to the back-end per visited URL in order get additional information like Web-of-Trust scores for encountered trackers. This may be expensive in terms of bandwidth, as well as unnecessary as reputation of trackers may not change that often. To reduce the number of requests to the back-end, we keep an internal client-side cache for tracker information, empirically setting each record's TTL to one week. Similarly, we cache the ground truth with statistics about relative privacy parameters, received from the centralized database, as well as EasyPrivacy lists for two days. Finally, we keep a server-side cache to avoid overloading APIs that are external to our infrastructure, such as those provided by the Web-of-Trust [30].

Invisibility of the Extension. Finally, we do not want trackers or websites to find out the presence of PRIVACYMETER in the user's browser. Previous research has shown that browser extensions may be discovered through a variety of methods [23,24], including detection via their DOM side-effects [25]. PRIVACYMETER has to modify a page's DOM in order to intercept the fingerprinting API calls. Specifically, PRIVACYMETER injects a script into page before any other script runs, which overrides all the fingerprinting APIs. To hide this DOM modification, we immediately remove the script tag after all APIs are patched and mask possible signs of the overridden functions, e.g., by ensuring that when the toString method is called, our extension returns the appropriate output as if the method was never overridden.

To calculate a relative privacy score, PRIVACYMETER must have information about the privacy practices of popular websites on the web. For example, in order to be able to provide a meaningful relative privacy score of a new sports page, PRIVACYMETER needs data about the privacy practices of other popular sports pages. Thus our architecture includes a central database with cached privacy statistics as presented on Fig. 2b. To ensure that our collected data remains up-to-date, we deploy a separate crawler, which runs continuously and analyzes a large fraction of popular websites. Given the flexibility of our design, a crawler is implemented as an automated browser with the same PRIVACYMETER extension installed, which is instructed to visit a range of websites and report the calculated privacy statistics so that they can be included in our centralized database.

3   PrivacyMeter's Evaluation

In this section, we report on the PRIVACYMETER's evaluation as a privacy preserving browser extension. First, we show the benefits of a relative privacy score, which is one of the key functionalities of PRIVACYMETER, comparing privacy practices across different website categories. Second, we test the performance overhead added by the extension to the daily browsing of users.

Relative Privacy Score. In this work, we argue that the ability to compare privacy practices of a website to privacy practices of other similar websites is a necessary function of a modern privacy preserving tool. First of all, it gives users more fine-grained options in order to protect their privacy. For example, with traditional blockers a non-technical user has only two options: either to block all the trackers, or to allow them all. In this case, when a content publisher deploys an anti-blocker solution [11,12,20], the user ends up with the choice whether to allow all tracking or leave the website. While savvy users may be able to find a third choice (e.g. whitelist enough of the trackers to be able to utilize the website), this approach is out-of-reach for the majority of web users. With PRIVACYMETER's relative privacy comparison, we equip *all* users with sufficient information to assist them in making a decision to keep on trusting the website or seek a different website of the same category.

Therefore, the next logical question that arises is whether different groups of websites and web pages have different privacy practices, making PRIVACYMETER's relative comparison between websites a useful and desirable feature. To answer this question, we compare the four main relative privacy features, currently supported by the PRIVACYMETER extension, across Alexa's 17 categories of websites, such as, "Sports" and "News." By crawling Alexa's top 500 websites per each category we populate PRIVACYMETER's database with a total of 6,580 distinct URLs on the 6,049 TLD+1 domains with known categories. Figure 3 compares the resulting box plots on the number of trackers and fingerprinting APIs.

One can notice that the distributions of the number of trackers and fingerprinting APIs indeed vary across website categories. For example, web pages belonging to the adult category tend to have almost no trackers, and hence lower fingerprinting activity, presumably due to the sensitivity of the service and with the goal to earn the trust of the users. Similarly, websites for kids and teens also deploy less tracking as a response to stricter privacy regulations. Contrastingly, news and sports pages (followed by shopping and recreation pages) tend to include more trackers, and tend to be involved more in fingerprint their users' browsers. At the same time, web pages belonging to the "Computers" category appear to not be utilized a large number of third-party trackers. This can be partially explained by the fact that sufficiently large companies, such

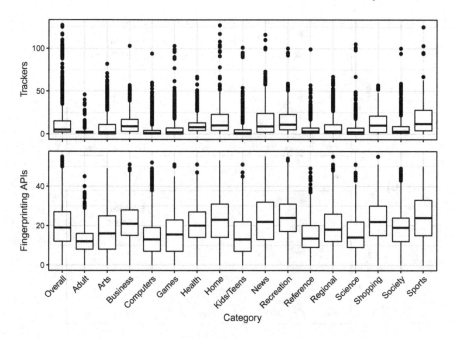

Fig. 3. Box plots for number of trackers and number of fingerprinting API calls per each of 17 Alexa's website categories, as well as the overall distribution.

as, Apple, Google, and Facebook, tend to utilize their own, in-house, tracking solution rather than rely on third parties.

In terms of third-party iframes and leaky web forms, only some distribution parameters, such as median, are different (see Fig. 5 in Appendix A). For example, news and sports pages clearly have more third-party iframes than other web pages. This could be because these types of pages rely on advertising for monetization and therefore are likely to be utilizing a large number of distinct iframes where ads are rendered. It is worth noting that PRIVACYMETER will count each loaded third-party iframe, even if it was substituted with another one. Next to these general trends, we can spot categories with strongly-pronounced outliers especially on the "leaky" forms box plot. For example, news websites have many outliers with websites containing up to 200 leaky web forms (our crawler counts each instance of a leaky form since the more present a form is on a website, the more likely a user is to interact with it).

Overall, our results support the premise that incorporating similar box plots to the PRIVACYMETER's interface and comparing privacy scores of a particular web page to them, can reveal whether the current website is an outlier or not, in terms of other sites of the same category.

Performance Overhead. In order to test the performance of PRIVACYMETER, we decided to compare it to Ghostery, a state-of-the-art commercial blocker which, according to prior work [19], detects more trackers than competing exten-

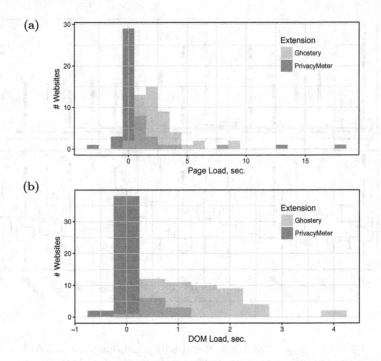

Fig. 4. Comparison of the performance overhead by PRIVACYMETER and GHOSTERY extensions based on top 50 websites: (a) overall page load overhead; (b) delay to the DOMContentLoaded event. (Color figure online)

sions. Ghostery, like PRIVACYMETER, does not, by default, block trackers but instead presents the list of detected trackers, which makes the performance comparison appropriate. We visited the top 50 websites according to Alexa's ranking with and without each extension. During each visit we recorded times of the DOMContentLoaded and Load page events. Each test was repeated 10 times with caching disabled in order to retrieve the average timing. For the measurements, we utilized a laptop with 8 GB of RAM, Intel's i3 CPU, Ubuntu 14.04 and the latest version of Google Chrome. We present the performance overhead as the time difference between the average page load time with an extension present and absent.

Even with the additional modules of PRIVACYMETER (described in Sect. 2), our extension introduces 0.138 s of delay to the DOM loading, and 1.217 to the overall page loading, while Ghostery adds 1.412 and 2.546 s correspondingly. Figure 4 compares the distribution of delays introduced by each extension for both of the load events. Note that the negative values mean that, for those particular websites, the overhead from PRIVACYMETER is less than the loading variance due to network conditions and system load.

According to Fig. 4a and b, PRIVACYMETER is faster for most sites. At the same time, PRIVACYMETER slows down only two particular websites more than Ghostery, in terms of the page load event. Namely, those are www.yahoo.com (12.7 s) and www.cnn.com (18.3 s). If in the first case we encountered two long delays out of 10 attempts, which increased the average of our measurements (the delays were likely due to increased size of remote content and previously unseen trackers). The second case can be clearly explained by the large number of trackers, fingerprinting calls, and third-party iframes loaded. Note that for the similarly resource-heavy www.nytimes.com, both extensions add more than 8 s of delay. It is worth pointing out that a 10 s delay does not mean that the user needs to wait for 10 s before being able to consume the content of the page. Browsers start rendering content immediately therefore users can start interacting with a website much earlier than the firing of the DOMContentLoaded and Load page events.

To quantify the frequency with which PRIVACYMETER queries our back-end for the information about trackers, we calculated how many unique tracking domains a user may encounter while visiting 10, 100 and 1000 different URLs in a row. For the simulation we analyzed the same 6,580 URLs of Alexa's top websites across all the categories. Table 1 presents the resulting statistics. If a user visits 100 different websites during a week (the life time of the client-side cache), PRIVACYMETER will make approximately 65 requests for the additional information about newly encountered trackers. If a user visits 1000 websites, PRIVACYMETER will initiate at most 495 batch requests.

4 Crowdsourcing

An additional component of PRIVACYMETER's architecture is the ability to collect privacy scores and privacy statistics of web pages that users browse. If users opt-in to our crowdsourcing mechanism, PRIVACYMETER will, after generating a page's privacy score, communicate that score and its individual parameters back to our central server. This crowdsourcing mechanism will enrich our database with entries for websites that the active users of PRIVACYMETER find relevant, and will help the crawler to keep available statistics up-to-date. Consequently, the accuracy of the privacy score will be continuously adjusted to provide proper, up-to-date values.

To protect the anonymity of users who opt-in to crowdsourcing, PRIVACY-METER does not collect any PII. Instead, for users who have opted-in, the extension reports to its backend the following privacy practices per web page: list of present trackers (their URLs), fingerprinting APIs called (and their counts), list of third-party iframes, and the list of "leaky" web forms. Our extension does not utilize any stateful/stateless identifiers that would allow us to reconstruct a user's session. Finally, in order to be fully transparent, the code of PRIVACYMETER is made available as open source and the extension itself does not utilize any obfuscated JavaScript code.

Table 1. Simulated numbers of encountered trackers while browsing popular websites

# Websites	# Trackers			# New encounters		
	Min	Avg	Max	Min	Avg	Max
10	4	65	188	3	8	10
100	154	271	365	48	65	83
1000	824	925	1043	397	445	495

Next to the improving of the tool itself, the ability to collect crowdsourced statistics about the privacy practices of websites will help to drive future privacy research that will benefit end users. For instance, the collected data can allow us to understand how privacy risks evolve and inform policies and future technical countermeasures. Even with our currently small user base (17 users at the time of this writing, most of whom are researchers participating in the Data Transparency Lab initiative [7]), we already see the benefits of crowdsourcing, which gives us ability to discover more trackers when considering other URLs of the same website in addition to its front page. Namely, these PRIVACYMETER users contributed privacy reports for an additional 7K URLs (belonging to both popular and less popular websites) which were not part of our crawling efforts on which 1,015 previously unseen tracking domains were detected.

5   Future Work

In terms of future work, our next step is to conduct user studies (using either online platforms such as Amazon Mechanical Turk or recruiting students from our institute) to quantify how much more helpful users find the output of PRIVACYMETER, compared to traditional output of existing browser extensions, such as, Ghostery. In this paper we decided to focus on the engineering and implementation challenges of building a privacy-preserving browser extension which are separate from followup user studies.

Next to user studies, we plan on adding detection capabilities for identifying malicious web clients. As with any system supported by user-provided data, malicious users can attempt to poison PRIVACYMETER's central database by submitting false reports. To the best of our knowledge no privacy browser extension deploys a client-side protection against that. We plan to mitigate this kind of abuse through a combination of client-side and server-side techniques including using proof-of-work algorithms [10] at the client side (to slow down automated submissions) and IP-address-based majority voting at the server side (to filter-out reports containing outliers).

6   Related Work

The modern market of privacy-preserving browser extensions is mainly represented by anti-tracking blockers [4,5,8,9,22,28,29]. While some of them attempt to provide additional information like categories of trackers, such as advertisement or analytics [8,9], the majority are general blockers, which just show users the list of discovered tracking domains. Similarly, to the best of our knowledge, PRIVACYMETER is the first browser extension to evaluate a range of privacy practices of visited web pages in a single solution, as well as to calculate a relative privacy score, comparing each site with other similar sites.

Leon et al. in 2011 evaluated the usability of nine blocking tools including Adblock Plus and Ghostery [14]. The study reports many issues revolving around the configuration and usage of these tools. Malandrino et al. also point out issues with user awareness and effectiveness of blocking tools [17]. As such, other privacy preserving extensions attempt to deceive trackers, e.g. AdNausem [1] automatically clicks on all blocked ads in an effort to confuse trackers about a user's true interests. Similarly, TrackMeNot [3] simulates dummy search queries, and BrowsingFog [27] obfuscates browsing history against extension-level trackers. Chameleon [2] attempts to unify fingerprinting features of the Chrome browser (similar to the Tor Browser), in order to break fingerprintability. Despite their benefits, none of the aforementioned tools provide feedback to users about the privacy practices of each visited website.

The work that is the closest to ours is the PrivacyScore website by Maass et al. [16], which deploys automated scanning of websites and allows its users to get security and privacy features for websites of their interest. A major difference is the vantage point of these two tools since, in our work, PRIVACYMETER is a browser extension running on the client-side and therefore having access to all of the content that a server-side crawler cannot access (such as content behind registration walls). Moreover, PRIVACYMETER's calculates a privacy score dynamically which means that the score that the user sees is always representative of the current state of the website, and is not a previous score from the last time that the site was crawled.

7   Conclusion

As companies seek to collect more and more data about our online activity, it is imperative that users develop an understanding of privacy issues on the web, rewarding responsible websites with their visits while shunning away from websites employing intrusive privacy practices. In this paper, we described the design and implementation of PRIVACYMETER, a browser extension (with a server backend) which aims to provide users with actionable information about a website's privacy-related practices and how it compares to other sites of the same category. We demonstrated that PRIVACYMETER's performance overhead is less than that of popular alternatives while offering more functionality. We have open-sourced PRIVACYMETER and we hope that, in addition to helping users online, our work can be used as a case-study for building privacy-preserving tools.

Availability: The demo of the PRIVACYMETER extension is available at Chrome Store: http://bit.ly/PrivacyMeter.

Acknowledgments. We thank the reviewers for their valuable feedback. This work was support by the National Science Foundation under grants CNS-1527086 and CNS-1617593 as well as by the Data Transparency Lab.

Appendix A

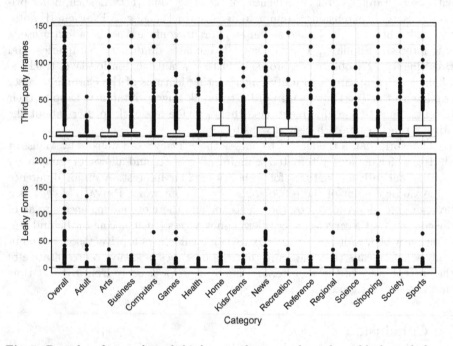

Fig. 5. Box plots for number of third-party iframes and number of leaky web forms per each of 17 Alexa's website categories, as well as the overall distribution.

Appendix B

The list of fingerprinting-related APIs currently intercepted by PRIVACYMETER:

window..phantom	navigator.product
window.callPhantom	navigator.productSub
window.chrome.webstore	navigator.userAgent
window.devicePixelRatio	navigator.vendor
window.domAutomation	navigator.vendorSub
window.domAutomationController	screen.availHeight
window.indexedDB	screen.availLeft
window.localStorage	screen.availTop
window.mozRTCPeerConnection	screen.availWidth
window.RTCPeerConnection	screen.colorDepth
window.RunPerfTest	screen.height
window.sessionStorage	screen.orientation
window.TouchEvent	screen.pixelDepth
window.webdriver	screen.width
window.webkitRTCPeerConnection	HTMLCanvasElement.getContext
navigator.appCodeName	HTMLCanvasElement.getImageData
navigator.appName	HTMLCanvasElement.toDataURL
navigator.appVersion	CanvasRenderingContext2D.fillText
navigator.cookieEnabled	CanvasRenderingContext2D.getImageData
navigator.cpuClass	CanvasRenderingContext2D.strokeText
navigator.doNotTrack	WebGLRenderingContext.getExtension
navigator.hardwareConcurrency	WebGLRenderingContext.getParameter
navigator.javaEnabled	WebGLRenderingContext.getShaderPrecisionFormat
navigator.language	HTMLElement.addBehavior
navigator.languages	HTMLElement.getBoundingClientRect
navigator.maxTouchPoints	HTMLElement.offsetHeight
navigator.mediaDevices	HTMLElement.offsetWidth
navigator.mimeTypes	Date.getTimezoneOffset
navigator.onLine	document.createEvent("TouchEvent")
navigator.platform	document.addEventListener("mousemove")
navigator.plugins	

References

1. AdNauseam. http://adnauseam.io/
2. Chameleon. https://github.com/ghostwords/chameleon
3. TrackMeNot. https://cs.nyu.edu/trackmenot/
4. AdBlock. https://getadblock.com/
5. Adblock Plus. https://adblockplus.org/
6. Chaabane, A., Ding, Y., Dey, R., Kaafar, M.A., Ross, K.W.: A closer look at third-party OSN applications: are they leaking your personal information? In: Faloutsos, M., Kuzmanovic, A. (eds.) PAM 2014. LNCS, vol. 8362, pp. 235–246. Springer, Cham (2014). https://doi.org/10.1007/978-3-319-04918-2_23
7. Data Transparency Lab. http://datatransparencylab.org/
8. Disconnect—Online Privacy & Security. https://disconnect.me/
9. Ghostery. https://www.ghostery.com/
10. Hashcash: Proof-of-work algorithm. http://www.hashcash.org/
11. Hruska, J.: Forbes forces readers to turn off ad blockers, promptly serves malware (2016). http://www.extremetech.com/internet/220696-forbes-forces-readers-to-turn-off-ad-blockers-promptly-serves-malware

12. Iqbal, U., Shafiq, Z., Qian, Z.: The ad wars: retrospective measurement and analysis of anti-adblock filter lists. In: Proceedings of the 2017 Internet Measurement Conference, IMC 2017 (2017)
13. Krishnamurthy, B., Naryshkin, K., Wills, C.E.: Privacy leakage vs. protection measures: the growing disconnect. In: Web 2.0 Security and Privacy Workshop (2011)
14. Leon, P., Ur, B., Shay, R., Wang, Y., Balebako, R., Cranor, L.: Why Johnny can't opt out: a usability evaluation of tools to limit online behavioral advertising. In: Proceedings of the SIGCHI Conference on Human Factors in Computing Systems, CHI 2012, pp. 589–598. ACM, New York (2012). https://doi.org/10.1145/2207676. 2207759
15. Lerner, A., Simpson, A.K., Kohno, T., Roesner, F.: Internet Jones and the raiders of the lost trackers: an archaeological study of web tracking from 1996 to 2016. In: USENIX Security Symposium (2016)
16. Maass, M., Wichmann, P., Pridöhl, H., Herrmann, D.: PrivacyScore: improving privacy and security via crowd-sourced benchmarks of websites. In: Schweighofer, E., Leitold, H., Mitrakas, A., Rannenberg, K. (eds.) APF 2017. LNCS, vol. 10518, pp. 178–191. Springer, Cham (2017). https://doi.org/10.1007/978-3-319-67280-9_10
17. Malandrino, D., Petta, A., Scarano, V., Serra, L., Spinelli, R., Krishnamurthy, B.: Privacy awareness about information leakage: who knows what about me? In: Proceedings of the 12th ACM Workshop on Workshop on Privacy in the Electronic Society, WPES 2013, pp. 279–284. ACM, New York (2013). https://doi.org/10. 1145/2517840.2517868
18. Mayer, J.R., Mitchell, J.C.: Third-party web tracking: policy and technology. In: IEEE Symposium on Security and Privacy, pp. 413–427. IEEE Computer Society (2012). http://dblp.uni-trier.de/db/conf/sp/sp2012.html#MayerM12
19. Merzdovnik, G., Huber, M., Buhov, D., Nikiforakis, N., Neuner, S., Schmiedecker, M., Weippl, E.: Block me if you can: a large-scale study of tracker-blocking tools. In: Proceedings of the 2nd IEEE European Symposium on Security and Privacy (IEEE Euro S&P) (2017)
20. Mughees, M.H., Qian, Z., Shafiq, Z.: Detecting anti ad-blockers in the wild. Proc. Priv. Enhancing Technol. **2017**(3), 130–146 (2017)
21. Nikiforakis, N., Kapravelos, A., Joosen, W., Kruegel, C., Piessens, F., Vigna, G.: Cookieless monster: exploring the ecosystem of web-based device fingerprinting. In: Proceedings of the 34th IEEE Symposium on Security and Privacy (IEEE S&P), pp. 541–555 (2013)
22. Privacy Badger—Electronic Frontier Foundation. https://www.eff.org/ privacybadger
23. Sanchez-Rola, I., Santos, I., Balzarotti, D.: Extension breakdown: security analysis of browsers extension resources control policies. In: 26th USENIX Security Symposium, pp. 679–694 (2017)
24. Sjösten, A., Van Acker, S., Sabelfeld, A.: Discovering browser extensions via web accessible resources. In: Proceedings of the Seventh ACM on Conference on Data and Application Security and Privacy, pp. 329–336. ACM (2017)
25. Starov, O., Nikiforakis, N.: XHOUND: quantifying the fingerprintability of browser extensions. In: 2017 IEEE Symposium on Security and Privacy (SP), pp. 941–956, May 2017. https://doi.org/10.1109/SP.2017.18
26. Starov, O., Gill, P., Nikiforakis, N.: Are you sure you want to contact us? Quantifying the leakage of PII via website contact forms. PoPETs **2016**(1), 20–33 (2016). http://www.degruyter.com/view/j/popets.2016.2016.issue-1/ popets-2015-0028/ popets-2015-0028.xml

27. Starov, O., Nikiforakis, N.: Extended tracking powers: measuring the privacy diffusion enabled by browser extensions. In: Proceedings of the 26th International Conference on World Wide Web. WWW 2017, pp. 1481–1490, International World Wide Web Conferences Steering Committee, Republic and Canton of Geneva (2017). https://doi.org/10.1145/3038912.3052596
28. uBlock. https://www.ublock.org/
29. uBlock origin. https://chrome.google.com/webstore/detail/ublock-origin/cjpalhd lnbpafiamejdnhcphjbkeiagm
30. Safe Browsing Tool—WOT (Web of Trust). https://www.mywot.com/

Security Analysis of Drone Communication Protocols

Christian Bunse and Sebastian Plotz[(⊠)]

Hochschule Stralsund, Zur Schwedenschanze 15, 18435 Stralsund, Germany
{Christian.Bunse,Sebastian.Plotz}@hochschule-stralsund.de

Abstract. Unmanned aerial vehicles (UAV) are increasingly used by hobbyists, companies, and the public sector [1] for a number of purposes. Although this is good, UAVs bear the physical risks of aircrafts as well as those of unmanned systems. Taken into account the exponentially increasing number of UAVs (i.e., there will be approximately 1.26 million UAVs in Germany by 2018), these risks are becoming more likely to occur. In addition to operational risks, there are also security related risks. UAVs are typically remotely controlled, which, in turn, opens ways for cyber-attacks (e.g., denial of service or taking over control). In this paper we demonstrate that taking over control of commercially available UAVs is feasible and simple. In detail, we examine and analyze a standard UAV communication and control protocol (i.e., the DSM protocol family by Spektrum Inc.). We discuss common approaches for attacks, minor observations, and associated security vulnerabilities of this protocol. Since the number of commercially available communication components is small, these findings can easily be ported to other protocols such as (HOTT, S-FHSS, FrSky, and others). Finally, we make some recommendations which, if implemented, will significantly improve the security of UAV operations.

Keywords: Drone · UAV · Security · Wireless · Radio protocol
Reverse engineering

1 Introduction

Unmanned Aerial Vehicles (UAV), commonly referred to as drones, are in widespread use throughout private, commercial, and military domains. According to professional journals[1] there is an estimation that by 2018 there will be 1.26 million UAVs only in Germany. Their use range from recreational purposes to tasks such as aerial surveillance or -photography/videography/sensography, as well as military purposes. However, as flying objects with a potential high risk of damage, it is important to understand UAVs security and safety risks as well as the potential impact such risks might have.

---

[1] http://www.drohnen-journal.de.

© Springer International Publishing AG, part of Springer Nature 2018
M. Payer et al. (Eds.): ESSoS 2018, LNCS 10953, pp. 96–107, 2018.
https://doi.org/10.1007/978-3-319-94496-8_7

Even high-end professional UAVs are based on known computing architectures that were not designed to be highly secure. This has led to a number of incidents where opponents claimed that they managed to force down hostile UAVs by interfering with control signals [20]. Such incidents have yet not be reported for private or commercial UAVs but these too are based on known components. Interestingly, vendors rely on the secrecy of the design or implementation as the main method of providing security for the system. Thus, attackers can use standard "hacking" tools to "easily" take control of a UAV in order to hinder it completing its tasks or, even worse, to create damage. Beneath UAV hijacking most UAVs collect and store data locally. Often stored data is not encrypted and even its transmission (wireless telemetry) can be easily overheard by third parties. Interestingly, the effect of hyping new devices (e.g., "Internet of Things" (IoT)) that are vulnerable to "standard" attacks over the Internet is true for UAVs or drones as well. As a consequence, there is an urgent need for improving UAV security. First steps have already been done by European and National aviation authorities in form of new laws. But, more research is needed that systematically examines security threats in current UAV technology and to define means for mitigating these threats.

This paper examines potential security risks of UAV communication protocols (e.g., AFHDS 2A, DSM2, DSMX, D8 or D16 [2]). In detail, vendors rely on frequency hopping, spectrum spreading, and key sharing (aka "binding") as active security measures. However, legally vendors can only operate on ISM bands with a focus on the 2.4 GHz band using communication approaches that are based on packet-based transmission. Thus, they are closely related to protocols such as IPv4, but do not use security measures such as cryptography. This makes them vulnerable against known attacks. We will demonstrate this vulnerability by hijacking a UAV (drone) using known strategies. In addition, we will provide some ideas on how the security of UAV protocols can be improved while keeping properties regarding latency and throughput.

The remainder of this paper is structured as follows. Section 2 presents a short overview on related work regarding the security (and safety) of UAVs. Section 3 provides an overview on communication technology for UAVs and especially provides some insights into common properties and structures of UAV communication. Section 4 proposes a number of approaches for taking over a UAV during flight. Finally, Sect. 5 summarizes the results of the paper and gives a short outlook on future work.

2   Related Work

In this paper, the acronym UAV is used to represent a power-driven, reusable plane or copter that is operated without a human pilot on board [3]. Unmanned missiles or bombs are outside the scope of this paper. Most UAVs have remote control and communication means. Control by wireless communication bears the danger of misuse. However, research on UAVs is mainly focused on autonomous behavior and control. [4] provides an overview of the field and identifies the following research challenges:

- Aerial Surveillance and Tracking
- Collision and Obstacle Avoidance
- Formation Reconfiguration
- High Level Control
- Hardware and Communication.

As mentioned, wireless communication with other cooperating UAVs and/or the ground is key regarding security aspects. The UAV to ground problem typically addresses questions such as "out of line-of-sight" or "long-range communications". Interestingly security issues and especially the security of UAV communication protocols is often neglected. [5] provides an overview on general cyber-attack methods and on networked systems that are then used to identify possible threats and vulnerabilities of current UAVs. In general one can distinguish between four major attack vectors:

1. **Hardware Attacks:** Physical impact by shotguns, trained hawks, EMP pulses, etc. Such techniques are used in the context of preventing attacks or interceptions to critical buildings or sites. This might also include a direct attack to a UAV in case of getting physical access to the device. For instance, during the maintenance, one can purposefully or inadvertently infect an UAV with malware or replace boards or ICs.
2. **Wireless Attacks:** Wireless attacks make use of the wireless communication channels to alter data on-board the UAV autopilot. The worst case scenario for this attack is an attacker who manages to break the protection of the UAV communication channel. Once this occurs, an attacker can gain full control of the UAV if the communication protocol is known. For example, it has been shown that the DSMX protocol is vulnerable to a brute force attack [12]. Specifically developed hardware and remote control were used to carry out the attack [19]. Unfortunately, the published material does not contain all the information needed to carry out the attack. In this paper, the available information was therefore used as a guide for carrying out the attack with standard hardware (see Sect. 4). The missing information on how the DSMX protocol works was taken from the implementation of the DIY Multiprotocol TX module project [15]. In addition, missing details of the brute force attack are presented in this paper.
3. **Sensor Spoofing:** Sensor spoofing attacks are directed towards on-board sensors that depend on the outside environment. Examples of such sensors are the GPS receivers, vision, radar, sonar, lidar, and IR sensors. An attacker can send false data through the GPS channels, or blind any of the vision sensors. The UAV autopilot relies heavily on sensor data for guidance and navigation, so corrupted sensor data can be very dangerous.

[6] identified additional threats to UAVs in an effort to have a better public discussion of realistic attacks that vendors need to take into consideration when designing their products. In detail, the authors implemented and tested several attacks and considered privacy issues regarding drones that are controlled by

WLAN (i.e., hobbyist class). They further advocate to apply known IT security measures to UAVs as well.

For a comprehensive list of additional vulnerabilities found on UAVs as well as attack tools and methodologies, refer to [7].

3   Protocol Principles

Wireless communication of UAVs is based on wireless radio protocols. We therefore will examine the typical structure and elements of messages of a radio protocol. Subsequently, we describe the processing steps that are carried out by the radio chip in order to send or receive messages. To send a message, the data must first be encoded and then modulated. The individual steps for sending a message are shown graphically in Fig. 1. The bit sequence of the message is hereinafter referred to as "*message bits*" and the bit sequence of the encoded message as "*data bits*". The **Frequency Hopping Spread Spectrum (FHSS)** method is often used to make data transmission more resistant to interferences.

Fig. 1. Sending messages

To receive a message, the described steps are carried out in the reversed order. The received signal is first demodulated and then decoded. The steps for receiving a message are shown in Fig. 2.

Fig. 2. Receiving messages

3.1   Structure of a Message

This section describes the typical structure of messages in a radio protocol. The following is an overview of the components of messages that are used in many protocols:

- The messages of most protocols begin with the **preamble**. The preamble typically consists of an alternating bit sequence (1010...10 or 0101...01). It is used to synchronize the clock so that the received signal can be sampled at the correct times. The length of the preamble depends on the protocol used.

- The preamble is usually followed by a constant bit sequence defined by the protocol, called **Start Of Frame (SOF)**. It marks the beginning of the actual data.
- The **length** field contains information about how much data is transferred in the current message. The value of this field is typically set automatically by the radio chip.
- In order to check whether a data packet has been transmitted without errors, many protocols contain a **checksum** field with a checksum. The recipient also calculates a checksum of the received message. If the calculated checksum does not match the received one, the receiver will assume an incorrect transmission and will discard the packet. The Cyclic Redundancy Check (CRC) method is often used to calculate the checksum. The calculation and checking of the checksum is typically handled by the radio chip.
- The bit sequence called **End Of Frame (EOF)** identifies for many protocols the end of a message. The bit sequence is determined by the protocol.

3.2   Encoding

After the previous section dealt with the typical structure of messages of a radio protocol, this section deals with the encoding of the message. Encoding describes the conversion of message bits into data bits, which are then transmitted via the physical channel. The encoding is done to make the signal more robust against interferences during radio transmission. A frequently used method is **Direct Sequence Spread Spectrum (DSSS)**. In this method, the message bits are XORed with pseudonoise (PN) codes (see Fig. 3).

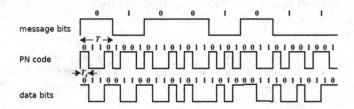

Fig. 3. Direct Sequence Spread Spectrum (DSSS) (modified, [8])

In the shown example, each bit of the message bits is encoded by four bits in the data bits. This makes it easier to detect and correct errors that may have occurred. The message bits can only be reconstructed if the PN codes are known.

3.3   Modulation

After the message has been encoded, it now has to be modulated. Modulation is the process by which the user data to be transmitted changes (modulate) a carrier signal. This can be done in different ways. For example, frequency shift keying (FSK) changes the frequency of the carrier signal. If a binary 1 is to be transmitted, the frequency of the carrier signal is increased (see Fig. 4).

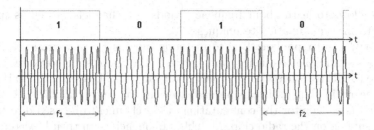

Fig. 4. Frequency shift keying (FSK) (modified, [9])

3.4 Frequency Hopping Spread Spectrum (FHSS)

Frequency Hopping Spread Spectrum (FHSS) is a method in which the carrier frequency is continuously changed. A unique sequence of frequency channels is determined by the receiver and transmitter during the binding process[2]. The receiver and transmitter then have to synchronize to ensure successful data transmission: For example, the receiver could wait for a packet on the first frequency of the negotiated sequence. After the receiver has received a packet, it switches to the next frequency in the sequence. The transmitter also jumps to the next frequency after sending a packet. The FHSS method makes data transmission more resistant to interferences: If a channel is occupied, the transmission is only disturbed for a short period of time. On the other hand, it becomes more difficult for an attacker to intercept communication if the hopping sequence is unknown.

4 Demonstration

This chapter demonstrates an attack vector to the DSMX protocol by Spektrum [12]. For this reason, we will first discuss the general steps to attack a protocol and take control of a UAV. Then the practical implementation of the attack and the results will be discussed.

4.1 Approach

In the following, we will first show how a protocol for controlling a drone can be attacked.

1. **Get documentation:** First the communication (protocol) between a UAV and its base station (e.g., a remote control unit or a computer) has to be analyzed. Although there is no real communication standard[3] the underlying basis boils down to four different radio chips: *A7105*, *CC2500*, *NRF24L01* and *CYRF6936* [10]. Identifying the radio chip and obtaining its freely available documentation is the starting point for all future actions. In detail, this

---

[2] The concrete procedure is laid down in the protocol.

[3] The Deviation project (www.deviationtx.com) lists more than 50 different protocols and subprotocols.

step allows to learn about frequency bands and channels as well as spread-spectrum or modulation techniques.

2. **Capture data packet:** Due to methods such as FHSS there is no single, easily identifiable frequency that carries data packets. A software defined radio (SDR) together with supporting software (e.g., Universal Radio Hacker) or the radio chip itself can be used to scan for active channels. A second option is to monitor the configuration of the channel to be used directly via SPI sniffing on the radio chip. Matching frequencies can then be determined by examining the documentation. Now messages can be recorded using an SDR and then be demodulated. The resulting byte sequence has then to be further analyzed (e.g., check whether it starts with the expected preamble). Data packets can also be received directly by using the original radio chip.

3. **Reverse DSSS:** If the DSSS method was used for encoding a packet/message, its PN codes have to be identified in a further step. Since, often a SPI (Serial Peripheral Interface) interface is used to control the radio chip, PN codes can be obtained via SPI sniffing.

4. **Identify hopping sequence:** In the next step, the actual hopping sequence or the algorithm used to derive the sequence has to be determined. In order to do so, either obtaining channel configuration via SPI sniffing or by SDR based sniffing and analysis can be used [11].

5. **Attack:** Once all necessary information has been collected, the final step is to attack (i.e., to take over control). This can be achieved, by a timing attack that makes use of the applied channel hopping procedure. In detail, data packets of the attacker are send shortly before the data packets of the legitimate operator. The UAV receives the attacker's data packets and immediately changes its frequency (due to FHSS). As a result, the data packets of the legitimate owner are no longer received and the attacker has full control.

4.2 Practical Implementation

This section discusses the practical implementation of the attack and the results. For this purpose, the most important properties of the radio chip used (*CYRF6936*) and the DSMX protocol are described first. Figure 5 shows the structure of a data packet for the *CYRF6936*.

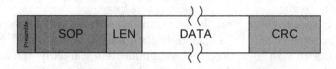

Fig. 5. Packet structure CYRF6936 [13]

The packet begins with a preamble, which is followed by the Start of packet (*SOP*) symbol. The SOP marks the beginning of the packets' payload (cf. SOF in

Sect. 3.1). In addition, it encodes the data rate for the remainder of the packet. The radio chip must be able to detect the previously configured SOP symbol in order to receive a packet. If this fails, no packet can be received. The *LEN* field contains the number of bytes transferred and the *DATA* part of the packet contains the user data. The *CRC* field contains a checksum to verify that the packet has been transmitted correctly. A CRC16 algorithm is used to calculate the checksum. The CRC16 is performed only on the length and data fields of the packet. Received packets for which the CRC check fails are still available to the application. The CRC16 can be seeded with a user specified 16-bit value [13].

Before a UAV can be controlled using the DSMX protocol, the remote control unit and the receiver in the UAV drone must be bound. During this binding, 4 bytes of the transmitter's radio chip ID are transferred. Since the binding procedure only has to be performed once for a sender-receiver pair, an attacker usually cannot intercept these packets. A binding packet has a length of 16 bytes. Table 1 shows the contents of a binding packet.

Table 1. DSM binding packet [14]

Byte position	Content
0–3	Radio chip ID byte 0–3 (inverted)
4–7	Radio chip ID byte 0–3 (inverted)
8–9	Checksum over bytes 0 to 7 of the packet
10	0x01 (constant value)
11	Number of RC channels
12	Subprotocol used
13	0x00 (constant value)
14–15	Checksum over bytes 8 to 13 of the packet

After the binding process has been successfully completed, transfer or data packets are sent to control the drone. The structure of a transfer packet is shown in Table 2. A transfer packet also has a length of 16 bytes.

Table 2. DSM transfer packet [14]

Byte position	Content
0	Radio chip ID byte 2
1	Radio chip ID byte 3
2–15	Data

Since the SOP symbols, the PN codes, the CRC seed and the hopping sequence[4] are derived from the 4 bytes of the radio chip ID, these must be known in order to be able to take over the drone. In each transfer packet, bytes 2 and 3 of the radio chip ID are transmitted. In order to receive a transfer packet using the CYRF6936, both the SOP symbol used and the PN code must be known. The DSMX protocol uses a predefined set of byte sequences for the SOP symbols and PN codes. Since the SOP symbols and PN codes are already known (see [15]), we did not have to determine them using SPI sniffing. Only eight different combinations of SOP symbols and PN codes are used per channel [15]. Which of the eight combinations is used in each case depends on the bytes 0–2 of the radio chip ID.

The next step of the attack is capturing a transfer packet. A brute force approach has been implemented for this purpose: Starting with the first channel used by the DSMX protocol (3), an attempt was made to receive a packet. For each channel, the eight possible combinations of SOP symbols and PN codes were tested. The receiver waits a little longer than a run of 23 channels would take to receive a packet (in this example 250 ms). If this is successful, bytes 2 and 3 of the radio chip ID can now be read from the received transfer packet. The bytes 0 and 1 of the radio chip ID are used as the seed for the CRC16 algorithm. These can now also be determined using a brute force approach: The CRC16 algorithm has been implemented for this purpose. The algorithm gets called with the data of the packet just received and with the possible values for the seed. If the calculated CRC value matches the CRC value of the last received packet, the correct seed (and thus also the bytes 0 and 1 of the radio chip ID) has been carried out. In the next step, the hopping sequence used has to be found. It is already known how the hopping sequence is derived from the 4 bytes of the radio chip ID [16]. Now that all 4 bytes of the radio chip ID have been determined, the hopping sequence can be calculated easily. In the last step, synchronization with the target system must now be carried out. To prepare for synchronization, the exact time intervals between the individual packets had to be determined first. For this purpose, the implementation of the DSMX protocol was temporarily adapted so that only one channel is used. This made it possible to record several consecutive packets with the help of an SDR and suitable software (for example the Universal Radio Hacker) and to measure the time intervals. During the attack, the program waits for the packet to be received on the first channel of the hopping sequence. If this could be successfully received, the following packets are sent shortly before those of the legitimate owner. To avoid a time deviation when sending the packets, the program attempts to receive the packet from the actual owner after every second packet sent. This corresponds to a resynchronization. As soon as the own data packets are sent shortly before the owner's packets, the attacker has gained control of the drone.

For the described attack we used a Banggood 4-in-1 STM32 module (see Fig. 6). This module contains a CYRF6936 chip as well as a CC2500, A7105 and NRF24L01 chip. The firmware of the DIY-Multiprotocol-TX-Module project

---

[4] In the DSMX protocol, the hopping sequence is a sequence of 23 channels.

has been adapted accordingly. The module was plugged into a *Frsky Taranis X9D Plus* remote control unit to take over the drone (Fig. 7). Table 3 shows the measurement results of the practical implementation of the attack.

Fig. 6. 4-in-1 STM32 module [17]   **Fig. 7.** Taranis X9D Plus [18]

Table 3. Results of the practical attack

Step	Duration
Receive transfer packet[a]	$10848878\,\mu s$ ($\approx$10 s)
Brute force CRC seed	$623649\,\mu s$ ($\approx$0.6 s)
Overall	$11645488\,\mu s$ ($\approx$11 s)

[a]This time includes the time to determine a channel and the combination of SOP symbol and PN code used. This time also depends on the smallest channel of the hopping sequence used, since the brute force approach starts with the smallest possible channel.

In this section we were able to demonstrate that it is possible to take over a drone in about 11 s when the DSMX protocol is being used. It can be assumed that this is also possible with other protocols.

5 Summary and Conclusions

Unmanned Aerial Vehicles are popular in many application domains and their sheer number is dramatically increasing. As aerial vehicles UAVs bear inherent dangers, which have to be carefully addressed. UAVs are typically remotely controlled using wireless communication protocols. Interestingly, most of these protocols are based on one of four physical communication units. Furthermore, the principles of protocols that make use of these communication units are either publicly known or can be re-engineered using a software defined radio (SDR). This allows the use of known attacks vectors such as man-in-the-middle or timing attacks to take over control.

In this paper we described and demonstrated an approach for attacking a UAV in order to take over control. We described an attack vector for UAVs using the DSM protocol family by Spektrum Inc. that is mainly used for hobbyist and semi-professional UAVs. In detail, we identified the used communication chip (i.e., a CYRF6936) and reverse engineered relevant protocol details. The CYRF6936 chip is commercially available and is designed to implement wireless device links operating in the worldwide 2.4 GHz ISM frequency band. The CYRF6936 is a fundamental unit that provides communication features. Thus, security means have to be implemented by the communication protocol itself. Interestingly a closer look onto the DSM protocol family revealed that although a kind of key exchange (i.e., bind procedure) is used, security is limited to a few bytes. By brute-forcing these bytes (i.e., the PN codes) the CRC seed as well as the frequency hopping sequence can be determined. By using a timing-attack (i.e., sending the attack packets shortly before the original packet), it was possible to easily take over control in seconds.

Due to the limited number of communication chips, and the known details of many protocols as described in the context of the Deviation project (www. deviationtx.com) this approach can easily be transferred to other protocols. Combined with a protocol analyzer using AI-technologies to identify the used protocol, attackers can take control of nearly any UAV.

In order to increase the security of the DSM protocol family, and in the long run of all known drone communication protocols it is recommend that transferring the secret key, negotiated during the binding phase, within the standard transfer packets should be avoided. This discloses parts of the secret every 11 or 22 ms. In order to prevent an attacker from receiving the transmitted packets using a CYRF6936 chip, the SOP codes used should not be known in advance and should depend on the negotiated secret. Furthermore, it is recommended to use the longest possible secret (at least 6 bytes). This makes a brute force attack considerably more difficult and ensures stronger authentication of the legitimate owner. Finally, it is recommended to use cryptographic methods. These should be publicly known and acknowledged. However, it should be noted that hardware resources are limited and that response times must be adhered. Thus, the right balance of security and performance has to be conserved.

In summary, we believe that addressing the discussed vulnerabilities and developing a "secure" protocol will help preventing the majority of software centric attacks. However, this may weaken defenses regarding site protection. Further work is necessary to investigate other attack vectors and protocols. In summary, we hope that our work will be a basis for future security analyses and efforts in the domain of Unmanned Aerial Vehicles.

References

1. Allianz Global Corporate: Rise of the Drones - Managing the Unique Risks Associated with Unmanned Aircraft Systems (2016). http://www.agcs.allianz.com/ assets/PDFs/Reports/AGCS_Rise_of_the_drones_report.pdf
2. Oscar Liang: RC TX RX Protocols Explained: PWM, PPM, SBUS, DSM2, DSMX, SUMD (2015). https://oscarliang.com/pwm-ppm-sbus-dsm2-dsmx-sumd-difference/

3. Pappalardo, J.: Unmanned aircraft roadmap reflects changing priorities. National Defense **87**(392), 30 (2003)
4. Ryan, A., Zennaro, M., Howell, A., Sengupta, R., Hedrick, J.K.: An overview of emerging results in cooperative UAV control. In: 43rd IEEE Conference on Decision and Control, 14–17 December 2004, Atlantis, Paradise Island, Bahamas (2004)
5. Kim, A., Wampler, B., Goppert, J., Hwang, I.: Cyber attack vulnerabilities analysis for unmanned aerial vehicles. Infotech@Aerospace J. (2012)
6. Valente, J., Cardenas, A.A.: Understanding security threats in consumer drones through the lens of the discovery quadcopter family. In: IoT S&P 2017, 3 November 2017, Dallas. TX, USA (2017)
7. Walters, S.: How can drones be hacked? the updated list of vulnerable drones & attack tools, October 2016. https://medium.com/swalters/how-can-dronesbe-hacked-the-updated-list-of-vulnerable-drones-attack-tools-dd2e006d6809
8. Slimane, B.: Spread Spectrum. http://slideplayer.com/slide/4800123/
9. Mietke, D.: Frequenzumtastung. http://elektroniktutor.de/signalkunde/fsk.html
10. Pascal Langer: Protocols details. https://github.com/pascallanger/DIY-Multiprotocol-TX-Module/blob/master/Protocols_Details.md
11. Shin, H., Choi, K., Park, Y., Choi, J., Kim, Y.: Security analysis of FHSS-type drone controller. In: Kim, H., Choi, D. (eds.) WISA 2015. LNCS, vol. 9503, pp. 240–253. Springer, Cham (2016). https://doi.org/10.1007/978-3-319-31875-2_20. https://syssec.kaist.ac.kr/pub/2015/shin_wisa2015.pdf
12. Jonathan Andersson Attacking DSMx with Software Defined Radio. https://pacsec.jp/psj16/PSJ2016_Andersson_Hacking_DSMx_with_SDR_PacSec_2016_English.pdf
13. Cypress Semiconductor: Technical Reference Manual. http://www.cypress.com/file/136666/download
14. PaparazziUAV: DSM. https://wiki.paparazziuav.org/wiki/DSM
15. Multiprotocol TX Module: DSM protocol. https://github.com/pascallanger/DIY-Multiprotocol-TX-Module/blob/master/Multiprotocol/DSM_cyrf6936.ino
16. RC Groups: DSMX Hacking. https://www.rcgroups.com/forums/showthread.php?1759502-DSMX-Hacking
17. Multiprotocol TX Module: Multiprotocol Module Hardware Options. https://github.com/pascallanger/DIY-Multiprotocol-TX-Module/blob/master/docs/Hardware.md
18. FrSky: Taranis X9D Plus. https://www.frsky-rc.com/product/taranis-x9d-plus-2/
19. Goodin, D.: Drone hijacker. https://www.youtube.com/watch?v=2YjQPPc5VW4
20. Kipkemoi, P.: Drone hacking - how safe is your drone? http://www.droneguru.net/drone-hacking-how-safe-is-your-drone/

Idea: Automatic Localization of Malicious Behaviors in Android Malware with Hidden Markov Models

Aleieldin Salem$^{(\boxtimes)}$, Tabea Schmidt, and Alexander Pretschner

Technische Universität München, Munich, Germany
{salem,tabea.schmidt,pretschn}@cs.tum.edu

Abstract. The lack of ground truth about malicious behaviors exhibited by current Android malware forces researchers to embark upon a lengthy process of manually analyzing malware instances. In this paper, we propose a method to automatically localize malicious behaviors residing in representations of apps' runtime behaviors. Our initial evaluation using generated API calls traces of Android apps demonstrates the method's feasibility and applicability.

1 Introduction

Current Android malware is implemented to leverage user trust in the Android ecosystem (i.e., applications, developers, marketplaces, etc.), and their desire to acquire new applications (hereafter apps). Nowadays, malware authors either graft popular benign apps with malicious payloads in a practice widely known as *piggybacking* [4], or opt to implement their instances as apps that offer fake, benign functionalities (e.g., a Sudoku with ten puzzles), concealing the malicious payloads residing in them [7].

Regardless of how apps are represented (e.g., API call traces or control-flow graphs), the majority of their representations is expected to comprise benign behaviors, while only the minority depicts the malicious ones. For example, if we consider API call traces as representations of the apps' runtime behavior, only a relatively small subset of calls in the trace should belong to the (grafted) malicious payloads. In other words, the malicious behaviors are usually surrounded by noisy, benign counterparts, rendering their detection difficult.

In theory, it is possible to detect such elusive malicious behaviors via cross-referencing app representations with repositories of previously-analyzed malicious behaviors. However, the process of gathering malicious apps and manually analyzing them to localize the malicious behaviors dwelling within them often spans years [4,7]. Consequently, there is a need for techniques to automatically locate malicious behaviors within representations of Android apps. In this paper, we propose a method using hidden Markov models to detect the existence of malicious behaviors in API call traces of Android apps and localize them within the trace.

© Springer International Publishing AG, part of Springer Nature 2018
M. Payer et al. (Eds.): ESSoS 2018, LNCS 10953, pp. 108–115, 2018.
https://doi.org/10.1007/978-3-319-94496-8_8

The contributions of this paper are: (a) we implemented a method based on hidden Markov models to automatically point out malicious behaviors within API call traces of Android (malicious) apps and evaluated its feasibility using generated data, (b) we make our implementation available to help researchers reproduce our results, and (c) we discuss potential enhancements to our method to be effective on real-world malware.

The paper is organized as follows: In Sect. 2, we discuss the notions and assumptions upon which we built our method. An overview of the design and implementation of our method is given in Sect. 3. Section 4 discusses the preliminary experiments we conducted to determine the feasibility of our proposed method. We conclude the paper and propose future enhancements in Sect. 5.

2   Preliminaries

To the best of our knowledge, the majority of efforts to localize (or extract) malicious segments from Android malware (e.g., [3,5,9,10]), rely on static analysis of Android apps, which might be countered via techniques such as code obfuscation, dynamic code loading, encryption, etc. [6]. Regardless of the techniques employed by malware instances to conceal their payloads from static analysis techniques, such payloads will ultimately execute and reveal themselves in representations of the apps' runtime behaviors (e.g., API call traces). Consequently, we focus on the runtime behaviors, particularly API call traces, of apps as our source of information about the apps' intentions.

As discussed earlier, in current Android malware, benign and malicious segments might be intertwined, which will also manifest in their runtime behaviors. That is to say, API traces of Android malware are expected to comprise calls issued by the benign segments of the apps along with calls issued by their malicious counterparts. We refer to API calls issued by an app's benign segments and malicious segments as *benign behaviors* and *malicious behaviors*, respectively.

There are two main problems with automatically localizing malicious behaviors from API call traces. Firstly, given the increasing utilization of triggers in Android malware, we cannot guarantee that the malicious behaviors have already been executed and, hence, are present in an app's API call trace. Secondly, assuming that a given API call trace contains malicious behaviors, we do not know which parts of the trace resemble such behaviors.

The former problem is, in fact, that of stimulating an Android app and monitoring its runtime behavior, which is out of this paper's scope. Consequently, our solution assumes that malicious apps have been thoroughly stimulated, and their corresponding API call traces indeed contains the malicious behaviors they withhold.

To address the latter problem–which is the one the paper attempts to solve– we build our solution on the following assumptions:

Assumption 1: *In Android malware, malicious segments usually differ from their benign counterparts in functionality and runtime behavior.*

Assumption 2: *Given a model representing all benign behaviors, we can localize malicious behaviors by finding segments (e.g., API calls in a trace) that are anomalous.*

Assumption 3: *Utilization of sensitive data and system resources often reveals the intentions of apps (i.e., malicious or benign).*

3   Implementation

In this section, we present the proposed method to automatically localize malicious behaviors in Android malware, depicted in Fig. 1 and discuss its different operations.

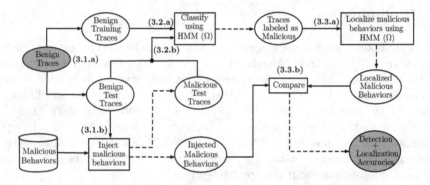

Fig. 1. An overview of the proposed method to automatically localize malicious behaviors from Android malware. Ellipses depict inputs/outputs, and rectangles depict operations performed on them. The blue labels refer to the section in which an operation is discussed. (Color figure online)

3.1   Data Generation

To assess the performance of our localization method, we need API traces of malicious apps, in which the malicious segments are known, which is usually not available. Consequently, we demonstrate the validity and feasibility of our proposed method using data we generated from API call traces of benign apps. The Data Generation module is responsible for generating such data that resemble real-world Android malware.

As discussed earlier, current Android malware comprises benign and malicious segments, which manifests in their API call traces with benign behaviors being the majority. Thus, we can generate a malicious trace by injecting malicious behaviors into presumably benign ones. We surveyed the literature for behaviors exhibited by common current Android malware families (e.g., Dogwin, Airpush, and FakeInst), represented the textual description of such behaviors into a sequence of API calls, and stored them.

To avoid unintentionally facilitating the process localizing malicious behaviors residing in an API call trace, we ensured that the malicious behaviors are not designed to be anomalous to their benign counterparts. That is to say, the defined malicious behaviors (a) use the same API calls utilized by their benign counterparts, and (b) are semantically valid (e.g., not reading a file before opening it).

The data generation process starts by randomly splitting API call traces (step 3.1.a) of benign apps into training (two thirds) and test (one third) traces. We wrote a tool that, given a probability (p) and a benign test trace, retrieves a random behavior from the *Malicious Behaviors* database, and injects it as a block into the trace with the probability (p), as seen in step (3.1.b). The larger the value of (p), the more likely the retrieved malicious behavior can be found in the trace. The decision to optionally inject the behavior multiple times into a trace was made to resemble the scenario of a frequently-executing code segment (e.g., in a loop or invoked via a `Timer`), which is common in contemporary Android malware [7].

3.2 Training and Detection

The benign training traces are used to train a classifier (step 3.2.a) that is (a) capable of representing all benign behaviors in the training traces, and (b) able to point out anomalous behaviors in a trace. In this paper, we use a hidden Markov model (Ω) to accomplish these tasks. A hidden Markov model is trained with sequences of observations that belong to states that are unknown to the model (i.e., hidden), and can only be inferred from the observations. Within this context, the states are *malicious* or *benign*, the sequences are API call traces, and the observations are individual API calls. If the model (Ω) is exclusively trained using sequences belonging to one state (e.g., benign), it will represent the probabilities of encountering specific observations at a particular point in time (e.g., the probability of encountering `android.app.Activity.startActivity` as the first API call in a benign trace). In essence, the trained model is a *probabilistic average* of all benign behaviors found in the training traces [8].

In step (3.2.b), we use (Ω) to classify the benign test traces and the generated test malicious traces as malicious and benign. This step can be considered the first step in localizing malicious behaviors by highlighting an entire trace as malicious. The next step would be to pinpoint the malicious behaviors residing within the trace.

Given a test trace $(T = [api_1, api_2, \ldots, api_n])$, the model (Ω) can calculate the probability $P(T|\Omega) = P(api_1^{t=1}|\Omega) \times P(api_2^{t=2}|\Omega) \times \ldots \times P(api_n^{t=n}|\Omega)$, which depicts the likelihood of the observations in (T) to be generated by (Ω). Since the model (Ω) has been exclusively trained using benign traces, the probability $P(T|\Omega)$, in fact, calculates the probability of (T) being benign. Intuitively, the lower this probability is, the more likely it is for the test trace (T) to be malicious.

To classify traces, we need to specify a value for the probability $P(T|\Omega)$ below which, a trace is classified as malicious. As seen above, such probability is a result of a series of multiplications, which leads to small, unintuitive values (e.g., 0.0000135). Hence, we can rescale the value of $P(T|\Omega)$ into its log-likelihood $\log P(T|\Omega)$, which yields more intuitive negative numbers (e.g., -100).

We refer to this log likelihood decision boundary as *threshold* (τ). In this case, the lower the threshold (τ) (i.e., larger negative numbers), the lower the probability $P(T|\Omega)$, the more likely it is for the trace (T) to be malicious.

Lastly, the length of a test trace affects the calculated log likelihood, primarily since it results in more multiplications that occur to calculate $P(T|\Omega)$. Given that different apps might yield API call traces of different lengths, we limit the length of all test traces during the classification phase to a maximum value (λ).

3.3 Localization

Based on its classification counterpart, the localization process (step 3.3.a) attempts to point out the most anomalous sequence of API calls in a trace and returns it as the malicious behavior. Given a trace (T_{mal}), deemed as malicious by (Ω), we recursively split it into two halves (T_{mal}^1) and (T_{mal}^2), and calculate the log likelihood for each half. The half yielding the lower likelihood is considered more malicious, and is, hence, further halved. This process continues until either the value of the log-likelihood seizes to decrease, or the length of the half reaches a lower bound value (e.g., three API calls). The half yielding the lowest log likelihood is labeled as the candidate malicious behavior in the trace.

In step (3.3.b), we compare, for each test trace classified as malicious, how far the behavior localized (in step 3.3.a) is from the one injected into its corresponding benign trace (in step 3.1.b) (i.e., ground truth). The distance between the two behaviors is calculated in terms of different API calls. The average distance across all malicious test traces is stored as *localization accuracy*.

4   Evaluation

To evaluate the feasibility of our proposed method, we ran the process in Fig. 1 25 times on a dataset of 1882 API call traces representing the runtime behaviors of benign Android apps we downloaded from the Google Play store. The collected apps were chosen randomly to represent different app categories. To obtain app traces, we deployed each app on an Android virtual device and interacted with it for 60 s using a random-based UI manipulation tool we developed, called Droidutan [1]. The API calls issued by each app were kept track of using droidmon [2].

To have a comprehensive view of how our method performs under different circumstances, we varied the insertion probability (p) to 0.1, 0.25, 0.5, and 0.75, the classification threshold (τ) to -100, -250, -500, -750, and -1000, and the maximum trace length (λ) to 50, 100, 200, and 300 API calls.

Table 1 contains the average classification accuracies achieved by (Ω) on the test traces after 25 runs with different values for (p), (τ), and (λ) (i.e., step 3.2.b). As discussed earlier, classification is considered the first step of localizing malicious behaviors. Low classification accuracies imply that malicious traces are classified as benign and vice versa. Consequently, the localization phase will operate on misclassified traces, ultimately yielding incorrect malicious behaviors.

113 of Malicious Behaviors in Android Malware   113

As seen in Table 1, the model (Ω) is capable of correctly assigning up to 99% of the traces to their correct classes (i.e., malicious or benign). We have noticed the existence of a direct relationship between the classification threshold (τ) and the API sequence length (λ), that affect the classification accuracies. We argue that long API traces (i.e., high λ) require larger thresholds (τ) to accommodate the increasing number of multiplications that occur in calculating the log-likelihood $\log P(O|\Omega)$. We also noticed that longer traces, the more the information (Ω) can infer about the app's behavior, which is reflected in the model's ability to classify them correctly. Lastly, we speculated that with low values of (p), the malicious behaviors will less likely be injected into the benign traces, making it more difficult for (Ω) to detect malignancy in such traces. However, the tabulated results show that (Ω) is capable of recognizing anomalous behaviors in an API call trace inserted with a probability as low as $p = 0.1$, with accuracies as high as $\approx$80% (i.e., with $\tau = -250$ and $\lambda = 100$).

Table 1. Detection test accuracies of achieved using the HMM classifier (Ω) using different insertion probabilities (p), thresholds (τ), and trace lengths (λ).

τ \ λ	p=0.1				p=0.25				p=0.5				p=0.75			
	50	100	200	300	50	100	200	300	50	100	200	300	50	100	200	300
-100	0.60	0.52	0.53	0.55	0.61	0.53	0.56	0.59	0.61	0.54	0.59	0.63	0.62	0.54	0.59	0.65
-250	0.49	0.79	0.53	0.55	0.48	0.85	0.56	0.59	0.67	0.85	0.59	0.63	0.68	0.86	0.59	0.65
-500	0.49	0.48	0.86	0.58	0.48	0.59	0.91	0.63	0.47	0.67	0.92	0.66	0.47	0.67	0.92	0.68
-750	0.49	0.48	0.58	0.86	0.48	0.47	0.70	0.92	0.47	0.49	0.76	0.93	0.47	0.56	0.76	0.93
-1000	0.49	0.48	0.47	0.64	0.48	0.47	0.55	0.77	0.47	0.46	0.64	0.95	0.47	0.45	0.64	0.99

In Fig. 2, we plot the average differences between the behaviors localized in the traces classified as malicious (in step 3.3.b) and the behaviors inserted into such traces (in step 3.1.b). For simplicity, we inserted only one behavior into a benign test trace. The average length of a malicious behavior is three API calls. Hence, we set the lowest length of a candidate behavior to be of three API calls. For every value of (p) and length (λ), we used the value of (τ) that yielded the best classification accuracy.

Considering all of the five behaviors we inserted into the test traces, the average differences with insertion probabilities $p = 0.1$, $p = 0.25$, $p = 0.5$, and $p = 0.75$ were 1.72, 1.58, 1.49, and 1.63, respectively. That is to say, our localization algorithm based on the model (Ω) localized the actual behavior inserted into an API call trace with an error margin (i.e., the difference in API calls), of 1.6 API calls.

We noticed that some behaviors are more difficult to localize than others because they comprise API calls frequently used by benign behaviors. This leads the model (Ω) to consider them as benign behaviors. Another observation is that, regardless of the value of (p), the highest differences between the localized behaviors and the ground truth were achieved at $\lambda = 300$. We argue that with (λ) values of 50, 100, and 200, the traces will be halved until two traces of length *two* and *three* will be left. Since we only consider API call blocks of length three, this increases the likelihood of localizing the exact behavior inserted into the trace. However, with $\lambda = 300$, the algorithm might wind up with blocks of length *three* and *four*. If the malicious behavior dwells in the latter block, there will always be a difference of one API call.

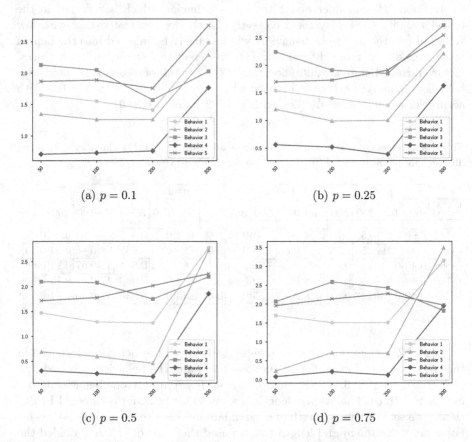

Fig. 2. The average (after 25 runs) differences (Y-axis) in API calls between the injected behaviors and the ones localized in step (3.3) with different insertion probabilities (p) and trace lengths (λ) (X-axis).

5 Conclusions and Future Work

Being able to automatically localize malicious behaviors enables researchers to understand the trends and techniques adopted by current Android malware, and perhaps build repositories or models of malicious behaviors to detect malicious apps. In this paper, we presented a method to automatically localize malicious behaviors found within runtime representations of Android malware viz., API call traces. To evaluate and demonstrate the feasibility of our method, we utilized generated data and showed that using a hidden Markov model, not only can we detect malicious behaviors with almost 99% accuracy, but we can localize malicious behaviors with the proximity of 1.6 API call. We plan on enhancing our method as follows. Firstly, we plan to run our method against traces of real Android malware and compare the behaviors found by our method with those manually extracted by researchers, such as in [7]. Secondly, in this paper, we assumed that malicious behaviors dwell as blocks of API calls within the API call trace. However, they could also be scattered along the trace, because the malicious behavior runs in a thread (e.g., a `Service`). To cope with this variation, we plan on enhancing our localization method that is based on bisecting the trace. Thirdly, using the malicious behaviors found and localized within real-world malware, we will train classifiers and verify whether they can detect malicious instances not used during training. Lastly, we will offer our implementation and findings to the malware research community.

References

1. Droidutan. https://github.com/aleisalem/Droidutan
2. Droidmon. https://github.com/idanr1986/droidmon
3. Li, L., Li, D., Bissyande, T.F., Klein, J., Cai, H., Lo, D., Le Traon, Y.: Automatically locating malicious packages in piggybacked android apps. In: Proceedings of the 2017 IEEE/ACM 4th International Conference on Mobile Software Engineering and Systems, MOBILESoft 2017, pp. 170–174 (2017)
4. Li, L., Li, D., Bissyande, T., Klein, J., Le Traon, Y., Lo, D., Cavallaro, L.: Understanding android app piggybacking: a systematic study of malicious code grafting. IEEE Trans. Inf. Forensics Secur. **12**, 1269–1284 (2017)
5. Pan, X., Wang, X., Duan, Y., Wang, X., Yin, H.: Dark hazard: learning-based, large-scale discovery of hidden sensitive operations in android apps. In: Proceedings of Network and Distributed System Security Symposium, NDSS 2017, (2017)
6. Rasthofer, S., Arzt, S., Triller, S., Pradel, M.: Making malory behave maliciously: targeted fuzzing of android execution environments. In: 2017 IEEE/ACM 39th International Conference on Software Engineering, ICSE 2017, pp. 300–311 (2017)
7. Wei, F., Li, Y., Roy, S., Ou, X., Zhou, W.: Deep ground truth analysis of current android malware. In: Polychronakis, M., Meier, M. (eds.) DIMVA 2017. LNCS, vol. 10327, pp. 252–276. Springer, Cham (2017). https://doi.org/10.1007/978-3-319-60876-1_12
8. Wong, W., Stamp, M.: Hunting for metamorphic engines. J. Comput. Virol. **2**, 211–229 (2006)
9. Yang, C., Xu, Z., Gu, G., Yegneswaran, V., Porras, P.: DroidMiner: automated mining and characterization of fine-grained malicious behaviors in android applications. In: Kutyłowski, M., Vaidya, J. (eds.) ESORICS 2014. LNCS, vol. 8712, pp. 163–182. Springer, Cham (2014). https://doi.org/10.1007/978-3-319-11203-9_10
10. Zheng, M., Sun, M., Lui, J.: Droid analytics: a signature based analytic system to collect, extract, analyze and associate android malware. In: Proceedings of the 12th IEEE International Conference on Trust, Security and Privacy in Computing and Communications. TrustCom 2013, pp. 163–171 (2013)

Idea: Benchmarking Android Data Leak Detection Tools

Claudio Corrodi(✉), Timo Spring, Mohammad Ghafari, and Oscar Nierstrasz

Software Composition Group, University of Bern, Bern, Switzerland
corrodi@inf.unibe.ch
http://scg.unibe.ch/

Abstract. Virtual application stores for mobile platforms contain many malign and benign applications that exhibit security issues, such as the leaking of sensitive data. In recent years, researchers have proposed a myriad of techniques and tools to detect such issues automatically. However, it is unclear how these approaches perform compared to each other. The tools are often no longer available, thus comparing different approaches is almost infeasible.

In this work, we propose an approach to execute static analysis tools and collect their output to obtain unified reports in a common format. We review the current state-of-the-art in Android data leak detection tools, and from a list of 87 approaches, of which we were able to obtain and execute five. We compare these using a set of known vulnerabilities and discuss the overall performance of the tools. We further present an approach to compare security analysis tools by normalising their interfaces, which simplifies result reproduction and extension.

Keywords: Data leak · Android · Benchmarking

1 Introduction

Security of mobile applications is a hot topic in both research and industry. Recent research has suggested that many applications in popular virtual stores, such as Google's Play Store or Apple's App Store, suffer from security vulnerabilities. There exist many approaches to automatically detect data leak issues (*i.e.*, situations where sensitive data may be leaked). Although taxonomies exist that catalogue and categorise such approaches [1–4], there is a lack of experimental evidence comparing the existing approaches.

In this paper, we tackle the following two research questions.

RQ 1. *To what degree are security analysis approaches and results in the domain of Android data leak detection reproducible?*

Anecdotal evidence from other domains led us to believe that artefacts and tools presented in research papers are rarely available online or by other means.

© Springer International Publishing AG, part of Springer Nature 2018
M. Payer et al. (Eds.): ESSoS 2018, LNCS 10953, pp. 116–123, 2018.
https://doi.org/10.1007/978-3-319-94496-8_9

We answer this question by reviewing the state-of-the-art approaches, trying to obtain their artefacts through various means (*e.g.*, using search engines or contacting the authors), and running them to obtain results similar to those originally reported.

RQ 2. *How do data leak analysis tools perform (individually and compared to each other) on a common set of applications?*

We run the artefacts on a set of applications with known vulnerabilities and report on precision and recall for each tool. We present a benchmark suite that allows us to easily run several tools on the same set of target applications and obtain reports in a normalised form.

We report on our findings by performing pairwise analysis on the tools, after running them on a set of synthetic applications with known vulnerabilities.

2 Related Work

There exists a wide range of related work. While a thorough discussion goes beyond the scope of this idea paper, we list those most relevant to our research.

Android Security Analysis Literature. Our literature review was mostly focused on works mentioned in the following taxonomies.

Sadeghi *et al.* present a large-scale overview of Android security analysis in general [3]. In particular, we used their categorization of security problems as starting point for our work [3, p. 12, Table 3]. Similarly, Sufatrio *et al.* published a taxonomy on Android analysis tools [5], as did Reaves *et al.* [2]. Gadient *et al.* have studied the prevalence of security issues in Android applications, including data leak vulnerabilities [6,7], and confirm that such issues are in fact common among Android applications.

Comparing Software Artefacts. In 2016, Amann *et al.* have analysed artefacts for detecting application programming interface (API) misuse violations [8]. Their approach is similar to ours in that they developed a framework for comparing such tools.

DroidBench[1] is a benchmark for evaluating analysis tools. Because vulnerabilities are documented in these applications, they are well-suited for the qualitative analysis we present in this work.

The work by Reaves *et al.* comes closest to ours. In their study, they use *DroidBench* to analyse results obtained from a set of seven Android analysis tools [2]. However, the only one in common with our set is *FlowDroid*. In contrast to our work, the evaluation lacks a comparison of tools amongst each other.

3 Classification and Selection of Android Analysis Tools

The process of reviewing relevant literature, identifying (potential) artefacts, and categorising them is straightforward. In this section, we briefly present the relevant steps.

---

[1] https://github.com/secure-software-engineering/DroidBench.

Literature Review. We started our process by taking a broad view on security analysis in reviewing related work. We focus on the works mentioned in the recent taxonomy by Sadeghi *et al.* [3]; we further reviewed two additional taxonomies to ensure that we did not miss any relevant approaches [2,5]. Based on those, we obtained and reviewed an initial list of 87 artefacts. Due to space constraints, we do not list them individually here and instead refer the interested reader to the mentioned taxonomies.

Next, we tried to obtain all artefacts by employing the following strategy:

1. review the paper, look for links or directions on how to obtain the artefact,
2. search online with contemporary search engines for the artefact, and
3. contact the authors and inquire whether the tool is available or can be made available to us (at most two requests by email).

In 60 cases, we sent requests to the authors. Of those, a staggering 49 remained unanswered.

We excluded several works for the following reasons. In four cases, the authors refused to give us access, either because their tools are commercially used or discontinued. Thirteen of the artefacts are not tools that can be executed but instead formal models. Nine tools are based on dynamic approaches; in this work, we focus on static ones exclusively. Four tools are not in the same domain, despite having been mentioned to be in the main taxonomy we used as a source [3]. Two additional tools are not relevant because they do not perform analysis on single applications and do not report data leaks. In one case, we failed to set up the tool due to poor documentation.

Selected Tools. After eliminating most of the tools as described, we ended up with a set of five tools for our benchmark: *FlowDroid, HornDroid, IccTA, IC3 (Epicc),* and *COVERT.*

FlowDroid [9] is a taint analysis tool based on the *Soot* and *Heros* frameworks. Its analysis is context-, flow-, and object-sensitive.

HornDroid [10] uses a combination of static and formal analysis.

IccTA [11] is an inter-component communication based taint analysis tool, suited for any data-flow analysis. *IccTA* uses both *Epicc* and *IC3* [12] as part of its analysis.

IC3 (Epicc) [12] detects inter-component communication with a focus on inferring values of complex objects with multiple fields, such as intents or URIs. It uses *Dare* for decompiling, and *FlowDroid* to generate an interprocedural control flow graph.

COVERT [13] is a static and formal security analysis tool. Its main focus is inter-application communication and escalation of privileges. *COVERT* performs value-, context-, and flow-sensitive analysis.

In the remainder of this paper, we present our approach to evaluating and the results obtained from analysing *DroidBench* vulnerabilities with these artefacts.

4   Benchmark Implementation

To easily compare the selected tools, we implemented a Java benchmark suite that allows us to collect results from individual tools. The benchmark then parses each tool's results and creates standardised reports and consolidates results, which allows us to easily review the reports, compare tools, and perform statistical analyses.

The implementation is straightforward. Pairs of runners and parsers correspond to individual tools. Runners handle setting up the tool environment and executing it accordingly, while parsers read and interpret the output for further (consolidated) processing.

To include a tool in the benchmark, one has to do the following. First one needs to set up the tool so that it can be executed from the command-line, and the output is stored on the file system. Second, one has to provide a runner in the benchmark that specifies how the artefact is executed (by implementing a single Java interface that provides information such as where resulting files and logs are stored), and third, provide a parser that creates reports (*i.e.*, objects holding information about a reported data leak).

The benchmark can be executed on a given Android application binary. Then, all relevant tool output files are collected and consolidated reports are generated. For each detected vulnerability, we list the class and method in which the leak happens, and the actual sink where the leak happens, as well as the analysis tools that detected the vulnerability.

An important aspect of implementing such a benchmark is extensibility. With a simple way to add additional tools—by implementing a runner for executing the tool on a given target application and a parser for obtaining the generated output—it is straightforward to obtain fresh results with a set of tools. This allows users to compare several tools on a level playing field. Furthermore, publishing the tools and their corresponding runners and parsers simplifies future evaluation and reproduction of results.

The benchmark and data are available online[2].

5   Experimental Setup

To answer the research questions, we use our benchmark to execute the five tools *IccTA, IC3 (Epicc), HornDroid, FlowDroid,* and *COVERT*.

For a fair comparison, one needs to make sure that the tools use the same lists of sources and sinks. Here, we use the *SuSi* tool [14] to obtain such a list.

We then configure all tools to use, where applicable, the same (i) sources and sinks list, as generated by *SuSi*, (ii) callback list, (iii) android.jar (API level 23), and (iv) apktool.jar (2.3.1).

As many others in recent research into Android security analysis, we use the set of programs provided in *DroidBench* for our analysis. We decided to

---

[2] https://github.com/ccorrodi/android_data_leak_detection.

Table 1. Raw counts of true/false positives/negatives.

Metric	FlowDroid	HornDroid	COVERT	IC3	IccTA
True positive	99	99	8	4	97
False positive	54	87	3	37	59
True negative	90	57	141	107	85
False negative	26	26	117	121	28

Table 2. Collected metrics for each tool as observed on *DroidBench* vulnerabilities. Bold values indicate maxima for the respective metric.

Metric	FlowDroid	HornDroid	COVERT	IC3	IccTA
Accuracy	**0.703**	0.580	0.554	0.413	0.677
Precision	0.647	0.532	**0.727**	0.098	0.622
Recall	**0.792**	**0.792**	0.064	0.032	0.776

select this benchmark because it specifically targets data leak vulnerabilities, and because individual vulnerabilities are described in text, thus providing us with a ground truth. This enables us to review the reports generated by our tool, and identify reports as true or false positives or negatives.

After running the benchmark with the normalised configuration on all *Droid-Bench* applications, two authors reviewed the obtained reports. For each *Droid-Bench* application, we proceed as follows. First, we record the vulnerabilities specified in the code (*i.e.*, the vulnerabilities stated by the *DroidBench* authors). Second, for each detected leak that corresponds to a *DroidBench* vulnerability, we record the tools that detect it (true positives), and those that do not (false positives). Third, for each additional report, we record the tools that report it (false positive), and those that do not (true negative). After processing 125 *DroidBench* vulnerabilities, we can report on each tool's precision and recall.

Because we have evaluated the tools using the same configurations and on the same dataset, we can also perform pairwise comparisons. We do this using McNemar's Test [15], which is a statistical test for determining whether, based on our observations, two tools are likely to report the same issues.

6   Results

Executing the analyses results in 269 distinct reports from the tools. We reviewed all reports manually and determined for each report whether it matches a vulnerability described in *DroidBench* and which tools are reporting it.

Table 1 summarises our results. What is striking is the poor performance of *IC3*, which reports 41 data leaks, of which only 4 are true positives. Furthermore, we note that *COVERT* and *IC3* only produce 11 and 41 reports respectively, a far cry from what the other tools report.

Table 3. χ^2-values from McNemar's test for each pair of tools. Bold indicates a statistically significant difference.

	HornDroid	COVERT	IC3	IccTA
FlowDroid	**9.94**	**10.56**	**35.29**	2.77
HornDroid		0.2	**8.53**	6.01
COVERT			**26.33**	**6.97**
IC3				**28.99**

Table 2 shows accuracy, precision, and recall for each tool. Here, recall is of particular interest, as it only includes *DroidBench* vulnerabilities in the calculation. We observe that both *FlowDroid* and *HornDroid* perform equally well on the dataset, reporting almost 80% of the vulnerabilities. However, as we will see below, the sets of reported issues do not match completely.

Both *IC3* and *COVERT* distinguish themselves from the other artefacts in that they report very few leaks. Unfortunately, this does not result in better accuracy or recall. The precision of *COVERT*, however, is high; 8 out of 11 reports are true positives.

It is worth to note that 113 of the 125 *DroidBench* vulnerabilities—or 90.4%—are reported by at least one tool. We think that this is surprisingly high, considering the wide variety of applications and vulnerability characteristics.

Next, we investigate how the performances of two tools relate to each other. We apply McNemar's Test [15] to obtain a measure that expresses similarities between two detectors.

A χ^2 value above $\chi^2_{1,0.01} = 6.635$ (which corresponds to a confidence interval of 99%) indicates that there is a statistically significant difference between the performances of the two classifiers. Otherwise, the null hypothesis (*i.e.*, that two tools perform equally well) holds with a probability of at least 99%.

Table 3 summarises the findings. Bold values indicate places where a statistically significant difference between two tools has been observed.

Most pairs of tools report different sets of leaks with a statistically significant difference. As McNemar's Test exclusively considers the cases where tools disagree, this means that for each pair, one tool is wrong more frequently than the other. However, according to the underlying raw data, there is no tool that performs clearly better than all others.

FlowDroid is less often wrong than any other tool. However, it is important to note that *FlowDroid* and *IccTA* perform very similarly; they disagree in only 13 cases. This is reflected in Table 3, as the corresponding χ^2 value indicates that there is no statistically significant difference in performance of the tools.

Similarly, the χ^2 value between *HornDroid* and *IccTA* is below the threshold.

As an odd occurrence, *COVERT* and *HornDroid* also exhibit a very low χ^2 value. This happens even though the two tools report vastly different sets, as evident in Table 1. In this case, McNemar's test may not be best suited, as it only considers the difference of the disagreeing reports, which, in this case, is very low. Nevertheless, the test is well-suited to compare classifiers in general, and, using additional data, constitutes a valuable metric in our analysis.

7   Threats to Validity

The benchmark we implemented may contain bugs that directly influence the results. To mitigate this threat, we implemented unit tests during development, and manually verified the generated output on a regular basis.

There may be vulnerabilities in the synthetic applications of *DroidBench* that are not reported as such. This may influence precision and recall of the tools. To mitigate this thread, we manually reviewed potential false positives (without finding any true positive vulnerabilities not documented by *DroidBench*).

Both *DroidBench* and *FlowDroid* originate from the same research group, so it may be possible that there is a selection bias that favours *FlowDroid*.

It is possible that we have made mistakes in configuring some of the tools that we tested. We mitigate this threat by only making minimal changes to a tool's configuration. Whenever possible, we use the tools as distributed.

Finally, the different publication years suggest that the original authors likely did not work with the same target Android version. Our choice to normalise configurations, in particular using the same sources, sinks, and Android version, may thus influence the results. Nevertheless, we argue that the threat is minimal, and that using the same configuration for the tools is a sensible choice.

8   Conclusions and Future Work

In this paper, we investigate to what degree static tools that assess data leaks in Android application domain are available, and how they work in practice. We report the progress from an initial list of 87 tools and approaches and describe the elimination process, after which we arrive at five tools that are suitable for our analysis.

We present a benchmark suite that easily allows us to consolidate results from the tools. To ensure a fair comparison, we configure the tools so that they use the same configurations. Furthermore, we apply them to the same targets, and avoid cherry-picking particular *DroidBench* vulnerabilities.

We observe that most tools suffer from a high amount of false positives and negatives. When we compare pairs of tools, they show, with few exceptions, statistically significant differences in their performances.

In our future work, we plan to use our benchmark suite with real-world applications and not just synthetic ones. We plan to also study the root causes of poor performance in the tools.

Acknowledgements. We gratefully acknowledge the financial support of the Swiss National Science Foundation for the project "Agile Software Analysis" (SNSF project No. 200020–162352, Jan 1, 2016 - Dec. 30, 2018). We also thank CHOOSE, the Swiss Group for Original and Outside-the-box Software Engineering of the Swiss Informatics Society, for its financial contribution to the presentation of this paper.

References

1. Egele, M., Scholte, T., Kirda, E., Kruegel, C.: A survey on automated dynamic malware-analysis techniques and tools. ACM Comput. Surv. (CSUR) **44**(2), 6:1–6:42 (2008)
2. Reaves, B., Bowers, J., Gorski III, S.A., Anise, O., Bobhate, R., Cho, R., Das, H., Hussain, S., Karachiwala, H., Scaife, N., Wright, B., Butler, K., Enck, W., Traynor, P.: *Droid: assessment and evaluation of Android application analysis tools. ACM Comput. Surv. **49**(3), 55:1–55:30 (2016)
3. Sadeghi, A., Bagheri, H., Garcia, J., Malek, S.: A taxonomy and qualitative comparison of program analysis techniques for security assessment of Android software. IEEE Trans. Softw. Eng. **43**(6), 492–530 (2017)
4. Tam, K., Feizollah, A., Anuar, N.B., Salleh, R., Cavallaro, L.: The evolution of Android malware and Android analysis techniques. ACM Comput. Surv. **49**(4), 76:1–76:41 (2017)
5. Sufatrio, Tan, D.J.J., Chua, T.-W., Thing, V.L.L.: Securing Android: a survey, taxonomy, and challenges. ACM Comput. Surv. **47**(4), 58:1–58:45 (2015). https://doi.org/10.1145/2733306. Article no. 58
6. Gadient, P.: Security in Android applications. Masters thesis. University of Bern, August 2017
7. Ghafari, M., Gadient, P., Nierstrasz, O.: Security smells in Android. In: 17th IEEE International Working Conference on Source Code Analysis and Manipulation (SCAM), pp. 121–130, September 2017
8. Amann, S., Nadi, S., Nguyen, H.A., Nguyen, T.N., Mezini, M.: MUBench: a benchmark for API-misuse detectors. In: 2016 IEEE/ACM 13th Working Conference on Mining Software Repositories (MSR), pp. 464–467 (2016)
9. Arzt, S., Rasthofer, S., Fritz, C., Bodden, E., Bartel, A., Klein, J., Le Traon, Y., Octeau, D., McDaniel, P.: Flowdroid: precise context, flow, field, object-sensitive and lifecycle-aware taint analysis for Android apps. SIGPLAN Notices, vol. 49, no. 6, pp. 259–269 (2014)
10. Calzavara, S., Grishchenko, I., Maffei, M.: Horndroid: practical and sound static analysis of Android applications by SMT solving. In: 2016 IEEE European Symposium on Security and Privacy (EuroS&P), pp. 47–62, March 2016
11. Li, L., Bartel, A., Bissyandé, T.F., Klein, J., Traon, Y.L., Arzt, S., Rasthofer, S., Bodden, E., Octeau, D., McDaniel, P.: IccTA: detecting inter-component privacy leaks in Android apps. In: 2015 IEEE/ACM 37th IEEE International Conference on Software Engineering - Volume 1, pp. 280–291 (2015)
12. Octeau, D., McDaniel, P., Jha, S., Bartel, A., Bodden, E., Klein, J., Le Traon, Y.: Effective inter-component communication mapping in Android with Epicc: an essential step towards holistic security analysis (2013)
13. Bagheri, H., Sadeghi, A., Garcia, J., Malek, S.: Covert: compositional analysis of Android inter-app permission leakage. IEEE Trans. Softw. Eng. **41**(9), 866–886 (2015)
14. Bu, W., Xue, M., Xu, L., Zhou, Y., Tang, Z., Xie, T.: When program analysis meets mobile security: an industrial study of misusing Android internet sockets. In: Proceedings of the 2017 11th Joint Meeting on Foundations of Software Engineering, ESEC/FSE 2017, pp. 842–847. ACM (2017)
15. McNemar, Q.: Note on the sampling error of the difference between correlated proportions or percentages. Psychometrika **12**(2), 153–157 (1947)

Idea: Visual Analytics for Web Security

Victor Le Pochat[✉][iD], Tom Van Goethem, and Wouter Joosen

imec-DistriNet, KU Leuven, 3001 Leuven, Belgium
{victor.lepochat,tom.vangoethem,wouter.joosen}@cs.kuleuven.be

Abstract. The growing impact of issues in web security has led researchers to conduct large-scale measurements aimed at analyzing and understanding web-related ecosystems. Comprehensive solutions for data collection on a large set of websites have been developed, but analysis practices remain ad hoc, requiring additional efforts and slowing down investigations. A promising approach to data analysis is visual analytics, where interactive visualizations are used to speed up data exploration. However, this approach has not yet been applied to web security, and creating such a solution requires addressing domain-specific challenges.

In this paper, we show how visual analytics can help in analyzing the data from web security studies. We present a case study of leveraging an interactive visualization tool to replicate a security study, and evaluate a prototype tool implementing visual analytics techniques designed for web security. We conclude that such a tool would provide a solution that allows researchers to more effectively study web security issues.

1 Introduction

Cyber attacks, data breaches and other forms of cybercrime are increasingly common on the Internet today, making an ever larger impact on our society and economy. To maintain the security of the web in the light of these incidents, the ecosystems of security practices and illicit operations warrant extensive analysis, in order to obtain an overview and gather valuable insights, which ultimately allows for creating better defenses. A variety of large-scale web security observations have been performed for that purpose [1,2,5,19]. However, while comprehensive reusable solutions have been developed for data collection [4,5], there are no such solutions for the subsequent analysis phase.

Open-source releases of data analysis code from recent web security studies [1,2] show that current practices for data analysis remain ad hoc and largely underdeveloped. This leads to duplicated efforts, and as analysis tasks may be labor-intensive, they take up time that researchers could use instead to focus on the security issues themselves. However, researchers have no choice but to develop custom solutions, as no comprehensive solution for data analysis specific to web security studies exists in the literature up to date. Creating such a general, reusable and performant framework would allow researchers to gain better insights into their large-scale data and expedite their research, ultimately leading to them being able to investigate and respond to more phenomena at a faster pace.

© Springer International Publishing AG, part of Springer Nature 2018
M. Payer et al. (Eds.): ESSoS 2018, LNCS 10953, pp. 124–132, 2018.
https://doi.org/10.1007/978-3-319-94496-8_10

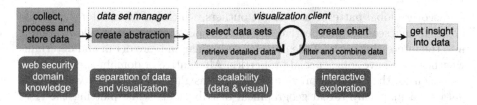

Fig. 1. The pipeline of a visual analytics approach to data analysis for web security, with below each stage the challenge it addresses.

Visual analytics is a promising approach to data analysis [10] which studies the integration of visualization and interaction into this process [16], using the former to leverage the increased data processing power of the human perception [10] and the latter to encourage data exploration. It has already been explored within cyber security in the domains of network security [14] and malware analysis [20]. However, it has not yet been applied for web security, despite its benefits to exploring vast data sets.

While the solutions from the other domains can serve as inspiration, they cannot be directly adopted for web security, as each domain has its own challenges that need to be addressed in visual analytics applications. In prior work [11], we presented an overview of four such challenges, and constructed a design of a visual analytics approach for web security, showcasing techniques that can address these domain-specific challenges. Figure 1 shows the pipeline of this design, alongside the challenges that each step seeks to solve.

In this paper, we explore the application of visual analytics to improve common analysis practices in web security studies. As an example of such an application, we develop a case study of using an interactive visualization tool to replicate a security study. Finally, we perform an initial validation of a prototype that implements our design, to evaluate whether its techniques are beneficial for analyzing the large web security data sets that are collected or publicly available.

2   Motivation

In order to gather correct and comprehensive insights from the large data sets that are collected for web security studies, it is important that the analysis process used can cope with the scale and diversity of that data. We discuss how visual analytics applications would be appropriate for this analysis, taking into account the specific characteristics of web security data.

Nowadays, web security studies routinely measure data for a large section of the Internet: Amann et al. [1] covered 193 million domains in their study of the HTTPS ecosystem, Englehardt and Narayanan [5] mapped online tracking through 90 million requests originating from one million websites, and Durumeric et al. [4] set up Censys for access to regular snapshots of the IPv4 address space. Through visualization, these large amounts of data can be represented within a single view, e.g. using aggregation. The visual representation makes it easier to discover global patterns and detect outliers, which are often interesting data points from a security perspective. Interactive operations can then allow zooming into the interesting parts of the data to study them in more detail and determine whether they have some special properties. Alternative or domain-specific representations of the data can provide additional insights: displaying server location data on a map may reveal geographical distributions, while plotting the IPv4 address space on a Hilbert curve [9] uncovers patterns in adjacent subnets.

The studies usually entail collecting different kinds of data and searching relations among them and with other data sets. Amann et al. [1] determined the correlation between the application of several security mechanisms related to TLS, while Vissers et al. [19] determined the distribution of sites with cloud-based security across the Alexa top 1 million websites. Multiple data sets can be explored simultaneously by placing their visual representations on a dashboard. By providing interactive combination of data sets, it is not necessary to consider possible correlations upfront: instead, hypotheses based on the patterns and insights found while exploring the data can immediately be tested by linking relevant data sets. Moreover, other data sets, including publicly available ones, could be imported to further augment the data that was collected. Interactions for making selections and synchronizing them across data sets allow for changes made in a certain view to automatically affect the visible data in other charts.

These examples show how visual analytics methods can be used in web security studies to support common analysis tasks, in order to speed up and enhance insight gathering and scale up the breadth of the studies. This helps researchers to have a more complete overview of web security ecosystems.

3   Case Study

As a case study of analyzing web security data using an interactive visualization tool, we replicate an experiment conducted by Englehardt and Narayanan as part of their large-scale study of online tracking on Alexa's top 1 million sites [5]. We used a custom web crawler to repeat their measurement of inclusions of third-party resources on those sites in April 2017, collecting 19.6 million inclusions.

The first step toward visually analyzing the data is making the inclusions data set easily accessible in the visualization tool. The data set is transformed to standardized data records and a context (a data type and description) is added, to remove the heterogeneity and ambiguity of data formats and sources. In order to provide interactive control of our crawler, we establish a link between it and the inclusions data set, which enables the dispatching of queries for additional data from within the interactive visual interface.

We can now use the interactive tool to start the crawling process. We load the top one million websites and their rank, whose data is sourced from a publicly available CSV file provided by Alexa[1], into a chart. The distribution of sites is shown in a bar chart, and by zooming into the desired range (through clicking

---

[1]   https://s3.amazonaws.com/alexa-static/top-1m.csv.zip.

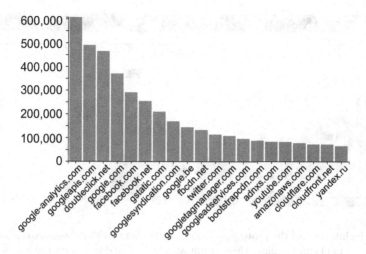

Fig. 2. A visualization of the third parties that are most included in Alexa's top 1 million sites.

or dragging) we could select e.g. only the top 100 000 sites. However, we want to collect data for all sites so we do not change the view. In a separate chart, we load the data set for the inclusions per domain. No crawling has occurred yet, so the data set and therefore the chart are empty for now.

Based on the shared `domain` data type, the tool knows that the two data sets are compatible. This, together with the link between the inclusions data and the crawler, allows us to interactively select and queue the one million sites from the Alexa data set, for which the crawler will collect and store the requested data.

We analyze the data with our tool once the crawling operation has completed, but could check on a preliminary distribution while it is ongoing. We load the inclusions data set into a new chart. Based on the `domain` data type, the tool automatically chooses a bar chart that displays the (sorted) aggregate number of sites that include a certain third party. Figure 2 shows the generated chart, replicating the original chart [5, Fig. 2].

By comparing both charts, we can see how tracking practices have changed in the 15 months between the original crawl and ours. In general, inclusions have decreased for the most popular sites. Google domains still serve the most included resources, with Google Analytics as the top domain. The top 10 has not changed much (differences are due to the merged `googleapis.com` and a localized Google domain), but in the next 10 we see more movement, with CDNs pushing out trackers such as BlueKai and MathTag. The visual representation of the data makes it easier to detect these patterns and changes.

We can continue exploring the data to obtain further insights: we can request more detailed data, the domains can be filtered or used as a filter with another chart to study additional properties, and distributions or correlations can be checked through combination with another data set.

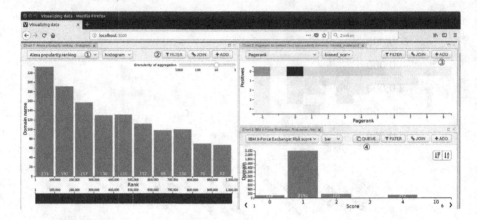

Fig. 3. The interface of the prototype visualization client, with a dashboard allowing to select data sets (1) and explore them simultaneously. The data set on the left is filtered on the items visible in the top right chart (2), where two data sets on the same set of items are combined (3). The bottom right chart shows data that has been interactively obtained using a crawler (4).

For their analyses, Englehardt and Narayanan created the OpenWPM platform [5], designed to simplify and automate data acquisition for web privacy studies. Our approach is complementary, as it provides interactive visual analysis of the obtained data, with both processes being linked in the visualization client. Moreover, the platform's crawls can be interactively launched and managed, which makes replicating studies straightforward (even periodically).

4   Design Evaluation

We implemented a prototype visualization tool, shown in Fig. 3, based on the design in our prior work [11] addressing the challenges we identified for bringing visual analytics to web security. We perform an initial evaluation of the prototype on three different aspects, which form proxies for evaluating utility and usability. More functionality makes a tool applicable to more use cases. For performance, a more responsive tool does not interrupt the train of thought. For productivity, requiring less effort to visualize data leads to more fluent exploration.

4.1   Functionality

We evaluate our tool's functionality using four criteria obtained from the surveys of open-source and commercial visual analytics systems by Harger and Crossno [8] and Zhang et al. [22] respectively: (1) data source support, (2) visualization and interaction techniques, (3) data analysis methods and (4) system architecture.

We hide the heterogeneity of data sources used in web security through a transformation into standardized records. This allows us to support displaying individual data sets from any data source. Two data sets of the same source can be combined interactively, however, supporting the composition of multiple data sets across sources is not yet supported. This would require a more complex data retrieval setup since data can no longer be combined at the database level.

The charts we add follow best practices from information visualization [17], in order to ensure correct interpretation of the data without requiring visualization expertise. Web security data comprises multiple data types, and currently our charts can display numerical and geospatial data. Graph and temporal data are currently unsupported, but our modular approach to charts simplifies extending the tool with appropriate visualizations. As for interaction, we support filtering and zooming to study data both as an overview and in depth [15], as well as linking and brushing [21] to enable synchronization of selections across data sets.

We have not yet added any interactive data analysis, such as statistical measures or data mining algorithms. These analyses would be interactively applied in the client but executed on the server, as the calculations need to be performed before aggregating the data.

We implement our tool using the client-server model, which places the burden of retrieval and processing of the raw large-scale data on the server. This reduces the processing power needed on the client and allows it to be web-based and therefore accessible across devices and platforms.

4.2 Performance

We focus our performance evaluation on how well the process scales with data sets of increasing size, as web security studies often yield large amounts of data. To achieve better scalability, we integrate default aggregation into our design, and we only request non-aggregated records upon explicit selection. We evaluate two performance aspects: the time needed to answer a data request, as this affects the responsiveness of our tool and therefore the exploration process [12], and the size of the resulting data, which affects the processing speed and transfer time. We test on data sets of 0.1, 1 or 10 million randomly generated items with attributes of either 100, 1,000 or 10,000 possible values.

For both the aggregated and non-aggregated approach, the time needed to retrieve the whole data set scales linearly with the size of the data set. However, the request for aggregated data is answered around ten times faster, leading to better responsiveness for larger data. Regarding the size of the response, aggregated data scales with the number of bins, but non-aggregated data scales with the size of the data set. For our test set, the latter yields a document that is at least six orders of magnitude larger.

4.3 Productivity

While visual interfaces are known to speed up analysis of cyber security data [7], analysts may avoid the process of creating visualizations due to it being difficult and labor-intensive [6]. We reduce this effort through automation of two phases: setting up the transformation of data sets to standardized records and selecting appropriate charts based on the data type. We evaluate the complexity of our visualization tool by repeating analyses using the original data from a study by Vissers et al. [18] on the parked domains ecosystem.

Data sets are transformed by executing code that describes data access and parsing. This code can be custom developed, which for a transformation to aggregated data requires 29 logical lines using the methodology of Nguyen et al. [13]; in total there are 28 such transformations. Automatically generating this code requires less configuration: for an SQL database 8 parameters are sufficient.

To quantify the effort of visualizing and exploring data, we estimate the number of actions and time needed using the Keystroke-Level Model [3]. Creating a new chart takes 4.0 s for four operations. Applying an operation to a chart (e.g. combining two data sets) takes 6.6 s for six operations. Combining these tasks into an analysis where two data sets are loaded, a selection is made in one chart and that selection is then applied to the other chart, takes 17 s.

4.4 Discussion and Future Work

Our evaluation shows that several design elements have a positive impact on the three evaluated aspects and therefore on utility and usability: abstracting over data sources expands functionality, aggregation improves responsiveness and automation reduces the visualization effort. Opportunities for further development lie in additional data processing and analysis functionality as well as further simplification of the visualization process.

In order to formally evaluate the utility and usability of our tool, we plan to validate it through a user study with web security researchers and analysts. This validation will allow us to more conclusively determine if our visual analytics approach is an adequate solution for enhancing their analysis workflow.

5   Conclusion

Through an overview of common analyses in web security studies and the development of a case study, we demonstrate how visual analytics can be advantageous for analyzing and extracting insights from the vast amounts of web security data generated and publicly available. However, domain-specific challenges need to be addressed in order to develop a useful and usable solution. Through an initial evaluation of a prototype tool, we show that techniques such as data abstraction, aggregation and automated visualization effectively tackle these challenges to enhance the exploration and interpretation of large web security data sets.

In the future, we plan to make our visualization tool available to the wider communities of researchers and analysts, as a platform for stimulating collaboration through shared data sets and analyses. In combination with easier (periodic) replication of previous studies, this opens up even more possibilities to analyze ecosystems and test hypotheses using the wealth of available data.

Acknowledgments. This research is partially funded by the Research Fund KU Leuven.

References

1. Amann, J., Gasser, O., Scheitle, Q., Brent, L., Carle, G., Holz, R.: Mission accomplished?: HTTPS security after DigiNotar. In: Proceedings of the IMC, pp. 325–340 (2017)
2. Cangialosi, F., Chung, T., Choffnes, D., Levin, D., Maggs, B.M., Mislove, A., Wilson, C.: Measurement and analysis of private key sharing in the HTTPS ecosystem. In: Proceedings of the CCS, pp. 628–640 (2016)
3. Card, S.K., Moran, T.P., Newell, A.: The Psychology of Human-Computer Interaction. Lawrence Erlbaum Associates, Mahwah (1983)
4. Durumeric, Z., Adrian, D., Mirian, A., Bailey, M., Halderman, J.A.: A search engine backed by internet-wide scanning. In: Proceedings of the CCS, pp. 542–553 (2015)
5. Englehardt, S., Narayanan, A.: Online tracking: a 1-million-site measurement and analysis. In: Proceedings of the CCS, pp. 1388–1401 (2016)
6. Fink, G.A., North, C.L., Endert, A., Rose, S.: Visualizing cyber security: usable workspaces. In: Proceedings of the VizSec, pp. 45–56 (2009)
7. Goodall, J.R.: Visualization is better! A comparative evaluation. In: Proceedings of the VizSec, pp. 57–68. IEEE (2009)
8. Harger, J.R., Crossno, P.J.: Comparison of open-source visual analytics toolkits. In: Proceedings of the VDA. SPIE (2012)
9. Irwin, B., Pilkington, N.: High level Internet scale traffic visualization using Hilbert curve mapping. In: Goodall, J.R., Conti, G., Ma, K.L. (eds.) VizSEC 2007. Mathematics and Visualization, pp. 147–158. Springer, Heidelberg (2008). https://doi.org/10.1007/978-3-540-78243-8_10
10. Keim, D.A.: Visual exploration of large data sets. Commun. ACM **44**(8), 38–44 (2001)
11. Le Pochat, V., Van Goethem, T., Joosen, W.: Towards visual analytics for web security data. In: Proceedings of the PAM (Posters) (2018). Extended abstract. https://lirias.kuleuven.be/handle/123456789/618030
12. Liu, Z., Heer, J.: The effects of interactive latency on exploratory visual analysis. IEEE Trans. Vis. Comput. Graph. **20**(12), 2122–2131 (2014)
13. Nguyen, V., Deeds-Rubin, S., Tan, T., Boehm, B.: A SLOC counting standard. In: Proceedings of the COCOMO. USC CSSE (2007). http://csse.usc.edu/TECHRPTS/2007/usc-csse-2007-737/usc-csse-2007-737.pdf
14. Shiravi, H., Shiravi, A., Ghorbani, A.A.: A survey of visualization systems for network security. IEEE Trans. Vis. Comput. Graph. **18**(8), 1313–1329 (2012)
15. Shneiderman, B.: The eyes have it: a task by data type taxonomy for information visualizations. In: Proceedings of the VL, pp. 336–343 (1996)
16. Thomas, J.J., Cook, K.A. (eds.): Illuminating the Path: The Research and Development Agenda for Visual Analytics. IEEE Computer Society Press, Washington (2005)
17. Tufte, E.R.: The Visual Display of Quantitative Information. Graphics Press, Cheshire (1983)
18. Vissers, T., Joosen, W., Nikiforakis, N.: Parking sensors: analyzing and detecting parked domains. In: Proceedings of the NDSS. Internet Society (2015)
19. Vissers, T., Van Goethem, T., Joosen, W., Nikiforakis, N.: Maneuvering around clouds: bypassing cloud-based security providers. In: Proceedings of the CCS, pp. 1530–1541 (2015)

20. Wagner, M., Fischer, F., Luh, R., Haberson, A., Rind, A., Keim, D.A., Aigner, W.: A survey of visualization systems for malware analysis. In: Proceedings of the EuroVis - STARs, pp. 105–125. Eurographics Assoc. (2015)
21. Ward, M.O.: Linking and brushing. In: Liu, L., Özsu, M.T. (eds.) Encyclopedia of Database Systems, pp. 1623–1626. Springer, Heidelberg (2009). https://doi.org/10.1007/978-0-387-39940-9_1129
22. Zhang, L., Stoffel, A., Behrisch, M., Mittelstadt, S., Schreck, T., Pompl, R., Weber, S., Last, H., Keim, D.A.: Visual analytics for the big data era - a comparative review of state-of-the-art commercial systems. In: Proceedings of the VAST, pp. 173–182 (2012)

Author Index

Printed in the United States
By Bookmasters